Acknowledgement

Have you known people who grow up in a good family receiving everything they want and need, yet they become unhappy adults who feel depressed or they feel the world "owes" them?

Yet others grow up in difficult circumstances and become happy, loving, even grateful adults. We wonder about this. Is it really not about what happens to you in your life, but rather how you choose to react that determines how happy you feel?

This is a true story about Twylia's life, experiences, and how she coped with them.

To my niece Debbie,
I hope you enjoy my
book. I wrote this for
my children + I got carried
away. I love you + always
enjoy being with you.

Twylia DuBois

I am writing this story about my life. My Granddaughter, Kelly, loves hearing stories about my life and asked me to write a story so the kids down the line would know about their ancestors.

I was born on July 25, 1930, at my Grandparents farm in Middletown, Kansas. Grandpa was George Allen Clinesmith, and Grandma was Lucinda Isabelle Bentley Clinesmith.

It was my Great Grandparents 50th Wedding Anniversary, George Edward and Mary Ellen Hodges Clinesmith. George was born 12/21/1851 in Chillicothe, Ohio. Mary was born 3/27/1880 in Wilson County, Kansas. They were married 7/25/1930 in Wilson County, Kansas.

My Mother went into labor so she and Grandma could not go to the party. I don't know why I couldn't have waited at least one more day. They seemed happy to see me though.

They named me Twylia Nadine Dexter. Mother & baby were fine. My Mother was Alpha Lucille Clinesmith Dexter from Wilson County, Kansas. My Daddy was Russell Oliver Dexter from Burt, Iowa.

A country Doctor delivered me. He got my name and information from Mother and tried to remember it but he didn't get it just right. He spelled the name different from Mother. The names were right, just spelled wrong, but I never did change my birth certificate.

My Grandparents lived on a small farm in an area then called Middletown. It was located between 3 other towns, Yates Center, Buffalo, and Coyville, Kansas. That's how it got its name.

Daddy and Mother were married January 8, 1927. My Dad had been in World War one. He was stationed in France during the war. He was ten years older than my Mother. When they met each other he was ready to get married and start a Family. My Daddy was 27 and Mother was 17. They were married 15 years.

One of my first memories was living in a house while Daddy was working for the Sinclair Oil Company in Kembro, Kansas. My Daddy worked for the Sinclair Oil Company for over Twenty Seven years. We had a house by ourselves. It was by a creek. My brother, Oliver, and I would play at the creek. He would catch crawdads in the creek and I played house on a real big rock. I would draw rooms with chalk. We were also near the Grocery Store. Most of the other Oil Field Families lived closer to the plant. My Grandma Clinesmith cooked for the oil field workers that were not married. They were living in Kembro, Kansas at that time. They were staying in a tent. I have a picture of them in front of the tent, the children were Aunt Elva Jean and Aunt Glenna.

We went to the Presbyterian Church in Madison, Kansas. Sometimes after church we would go to Guy and Lola Mayes for dinner. We kind of took turns going to each other's house after church. They were our relation but I had a hard time figuring how they were relation.

Grandma's parents were Jeffrey William Bentley from Yorktown, Indiana. He was born May 19, 1846. He married Almeda Jane Shelton in 1871. They had 9 children. There were five children in the family that lived to be grown.

Melissa Clementine Bentley married Jerry Mayes of Buffalo, Kansas. [Melissa was Guy Mayes Mother.]
Julie Pearl married Charley Clay of Skiatook, Oklahoma.
Almeda Jane married George Grant Mayes, of Buffalo, Kansas
Charles Wesley Bentley married Violet Pearl Clinesmith.
Lucinda Isabelle Bentley married George Allen Clinesmith of Middletown, Kansas. I only knew Great Aunt Pearl, Great Aunt Jane, and Great Aunt Violet, my Grandpa's sister.

My Grandma Lucinda [She went by Cindy], Melissa, Pearl and Jane were all sisters. These were the ones that I knew growing up.

We had a double marriage in the family. Charley Bentley, Grandma Lucinda's brother, married Violet Clinesmith Bentley, Grandma Lucinda Bentley married Violets brother, Grandpa Allen Clinesmith.

I have a picture of my Grandma Lucinda, Great Grandparents, Mary, George, my Grandfather George Allen, my Mother Lucille, my Daddy Russell and Oliver Dexter my brother.

1930

The picture was taken just before I was born in 1930. My brother was one year and eleven months old.

Anyway back to Guy and Lola. They had three children, Melva the oldest, Ronald, Oliver's age, and Otha Carol, my age. We all got along well together.

Oliver and I stayed over night with the Mayes after church. The next morning they gave us eggs for breakfast. I like the runny yellow part of the egg and I like the cooked white part of the egg, but I do not like the hard yellow under the runny part of the yellow. I did not want to eat it but Guy told me to eat it before I could leave the table. I love deviled eggs, and I like scrambled eggs. But I still do not like a fried egg.

One time Uncle Carl, My Mother's brother, gave me a baton. I told Otha Carol that I got a baton. She thought it was great. I taught myself how to twirl it. Otha and her family came to see us later and she was twirling in their school band. Needless to say she had gotten lessons and really knew how. She showed me how good she was and I just about turned green with envy. No one taught me so I couldn't do it nearly as good as she could.

Uncle Carl, my Mother's brother, taught Music in Fort Scott, Kansas. He gave Oliver a Cornet. He learned to play it pretty good while in High School. Uncle Carl gave me a Clarinet. I never had anyone to give me lessons so I never learned to play it very well. Grandma played the piano and taught me a little music, so I learned how to play a little. Living in the country I could never get in a band any way. We were 14 miles from my school in Fredonia. Many years later Carol played it in school, and Kelly played a little. I don't think either one actually played in a band. I still have the Clarinet. Uncle Carl said to never sell it because it was better than the wooden clarinets because it had a better tone.

Aunt Elva Jean, Mother's sister, told me that Mom and Daddy played bridge a lot. They had a lot of friends in Kembro. I was just too small then to remember the friends. She told me this about my parents after I told her I loved to play bridge.

I remember I liked to rock my Daddy. He would sit on my lap and I would rock him, not realizing that he had to be bracing himself so he wouldn't squash me. He was also doing the rocking. I couldn't reach the floor. I have two pictures of Oliver and I while we lived in Kembro when I was two and when I was five.

One day we had a big snow. All the kids were playing outside. One of the kids told me to lick a metal pole. It tasted good. Of course I did and got my tongue stuck. I couldn't get loose. I cried and someone finally got their Mother. She brought some water out and poured it on the pole and got me loose. This was Guys brother's wife. They had a girl Mildred. She was my age and we played together sometimes.

1932
Oliver & Twylia Dexter

Grandma and Grandpa Clinesmith left the farm and moved to Kembro while Mom and Daddy were living there. Grandma was a good cook and she was hired to cook for the single men that lived there.

Daddy got notice that we were being transferred to Texas. After Mother and Daddy were transferred, Grandma and Grandpa returned to the farm in Middletown, Kansas.

We took a nice vacation to see all his family before we moved. We visited Grandma Matilda Dexter in Burt, Iowa. We visited each of his brothers and sisters in their homes. They lived in several different states, Minnesota, Iowa, and Missouri. It was a nice trip but we had to go and get settled in Texas.

We lived in several different towns. I believe it was Overton, Texas that we lived by a big open field. The kids all played there. One time we were playing ball and one of the black kids was looking around to see who he could throw the ball to and I hollered, "Me, I am open." He paid no attention. So I asked a little white boy what his name was! He said we just call him snowball. So I called again, "Snowball, throw me the ball." Every black kid started after me. It scared me so I ran home. I was about 5 or 6 at the time and had never lived by a black person before. I learned quickly not to ever call a black kid snowball again. Sometimes Mom would treat the kids with a drink called Kool-Aid. I was always proud of her when she did that.

We went on a vacation back to Kansas to visit Grandma and Grandpa Clinesmith in Middletown. While we were there we went to visit Glenna in Parsons, Kansas at the hospital where she lived. We had a big picnic at the park. I was eight at that time. We took a Family picture of Mom, Daddy, Oliver and I. That was the only picture I have ever had of just my Family.

We also visited Uncle Carl and Aunt Oka in Fort Scott, Kansas. Uncle Carl took a tape of all of us talking. He started with Daddy. Daddy said, "Well, Here we are back in old Kansas now. We are trying to visit as many relatives as much as we can." That is all I can remember that Daddy said. Uncle Carl asked me to sing something on the tape. I sang the song, "Mires e dotes", and then Oliver played his cornet. Everybody talked. I kept the tape for many years, I can still hear Daddy talking, but as time passed I can't remember who has the tape now.

Years later I had a good talk with Aunt Oka. We were talking about our names, I told her my middle name was Nadine but I didn't like it very much. She said she never tells her middle name. I asked her why? She said because everyone laughs if she tells them. That made me real curious, she finally told me her name was "Oka Ola". I couldn't help it, I laughed.

We moved to another town called Taft, Texas. I think I was about 6, and it was in Taft that I started school. It was close to Corpus Christi, Texas. I liked it there because we were close to the ocean.

One day we went to spend the day and a baby Octopus washed up to the shore. Someone put it in a low tank with water so everyone could see it. We went to the ocean quite often to swim and picnic. Daddy rented us floats. It was fun to walk out deeper and get on the float and ride back to shore. My Daddy played with us in the ocean but Mother usually sun tanned on the beach.

While we lived in Taft my brother Oliver and I went to the Saturday shows. My Brother did not like for me to go because sometimes I would get scared at some of the shows and cry. He would have to take me home and was mad at me the whole way. That was only on the scary shows.

Another memory I had living in Taft was our big tree. The people that lived there before us built a tree house. It was just a pretty big board across some limbs, with boards nailed on the tree. We called that our ladder. I loved it. Once in a while we would have a fuss with the kids next door about whose tree house it was. Some of the branches were over their yard. Usually we made up and just enjoyed playing together.

I always seemed to have things happen to me. One time we were playing hide and go seek. I was hiding behind some scrubs, until I realized that I was on an ant hill. I ran in the house and Mom quickly put water in the bath tub and washed the ants off of me. I had some welts for a while where the ants bit me.

One time I had a balloon collection. I strung them across my bedroom on a string. I found one in my folk's bedroom. I blew it up and added it to my string. Later my Mom took it down; she said it didn't look pretty like the others. Later I found out that it was a condom.

This is a picture of me and Grandpa's horses. He had a different way of watering them. This was an old washtub propped up on some wood legs. We only had two horses. They were work horses but sometimes we rode them.

One time I was going to the mail box to get the mail. I asked Grandpa if I could ride one of the horses. He said yes but watch him because he tries to turn in at every road. I was watching the roads but the horse turned into a small path and I didn't expect that so I fell off the horse. We did not have a saddle, I was riding bare back. I held on to the rains so the horse could not leave me and hollered for help.

My brother heard me and came running. When he got to me, I started laughing. He thought I was tricking him and he got on the horse and started home. I started crying and told him I could not walk. So he came back. He put me on the horse and we rode back to the house. They took me to the Doctor and got an x-ray. I had broken my ankle.

I didn't have a bicycle so I would ride Oliver's. It was a boys bicycle. I would ride with one leg under the bar, so I was a little one sided. One time I took off on his bicycle and he was chasing me. I was watching him and ran in a big ditch. I fell on a big pipe and cut under my chin. I had to get 7 stitches in it. I still have that scar.

My Grandparents came down to Taft for Christmas when I was 8. I was sleeping with my Grandmother. I woke up real early and ran out to see if I got my bicycle. That was the main thing that I wanted. It was still dark. I looked and looked but the only bicycle I could see was my brothers that they had fixed up. I went to bed crying, Grandma asked what the matter was. I told her I didn't get my bicycle. She said go back to sleep, maybe Santa was not through yet. The morning came and sure enough I had my bicycle. It was just behind my brothers. I couldn't wait to ride my bicycle. They painted and fixed his bicycle so it looked good again. I rode around awhile then I asked Daddy if he wanted to ride with me. He agreed so I took him for a ride. I was a Daddy's girl.

We started to school in Taft. I don't remember much about going to school there. But I do know when I was going to be in the 5th grade my brother and I went to visit my Mothers folks in Kansas during the summer vacation.

My Grandparents had an old Studebaker car. I thought it was kind of fun. When we went to town my brother would hide down on the seat if he saw someone that he knew. My Grandpa drove with both hands on the steering wheel and drove pretty slow. People would always pass us. We were used to my Daddy's driving. Daddy usually drove pretty fast; he always had a new car. He bought one every two years.

One time we were going to Fredonia to town and when we got to the River Bridge we met the school bus. Grandpa got excited and just ran into the guard rail on the side of the bridge to stop the car. Oliver jumped out of the school bus and said, "Now what has he done?" I guess there was no big damage because we waited for the school bus to go on, then backed up and went on to Fredonia.

Grandpa Clinesmith

July 25, 1941

Twylia's 11th Birthday

I really liked my Grandpa. He would cut the wood with an axe that he had to swing and hit the wood pieces. We burned the wood in the stoves to cook on and to keep warm by. He had a stroke one day and from then on he would saw the wood on his knees.

He always used one of those long saws. Grandpa would be on one side of the wood and I would push and pull the long saw to help cut the wood on the other side. Then I would help carry it into the house. Grandpa had a great sense of humor and he was fun to work and visit with.

I had my eleventh birthday at Grandma's. She let me have a Birthday Party. This is a picture of the seven of us in the yard. I was the fifth one across. We look like rag muffins. I remember Betty was the oldest, then Barbara, and Beverly Beck. The 3rd one in the picture was Margaret. I can't remember the others. The Beck Family had two older boys. All their names started with a B.

ASSAILANT SHOOTS WICHITANS

LUCILE DEXTER, 31, above left and Robert H. McCamon, 40, above right, suffered gunshot wounds today at 3 a. m. when they were fired on by an assailant who crashed through the door of the apartment they were occupying at 315 South Water. Below is Russell O. Dexter, 41, 415 LaClede, estranged husband of Lucile Dexter, object of a widespread search who police suspect as the assailant. Mrs. Dexter is in serious condition in St. Francis hospital suffering bullet wounds in the left thigh and hand and a severe head injury. McCamon, also in St. Francis hospital, is in less serious condition suffering a bullet wound to the left shoulder.

When it was time to go back home to school in Texas, my folks said to go ahead and start school in Kansas. I found out later they were having family problems. Mom began to run around with this woman that Daddy did not approve of. I guess both of the women started running around with some other men while daddy was working.

Sometimes I would feel a little sorry for myself. I felt that Mother and Daddy just gave us away because they didn't want us anymore. They both kept telling us that they loved us, but left us anyway. That feeling stayed with me for several years. I don't

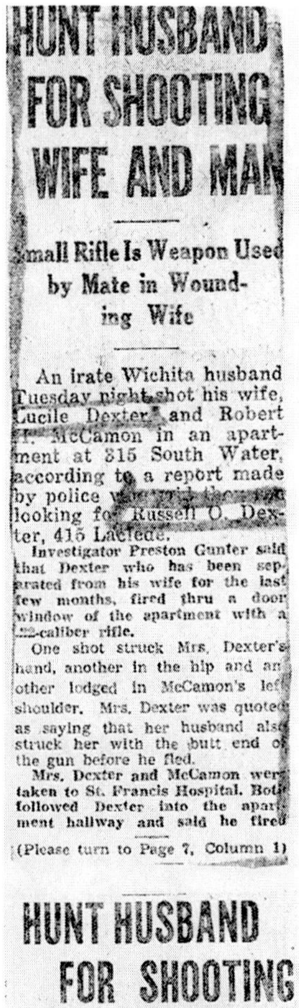

HUNT HUSBAND FOR SHOOTING WIFE AND MAN

Small Rifle Is Weapon Used by Mate in Wounding Wife

An irate Wichita husband Tuesday night shot his wife, Lucile Dexter, and Robert F. McCamon in an apartment at 315 South Water, according to a report made by police [illegible] looking for Russell O. Dexter, 415 Laclede.

Investigator Preston Gunter said that Dexter who has been separated from his wife for the last few months, fired thru a door window of the apartment with a 22-caliber rifle.

One shot struck Mrs. Dexter's hand, another in the hip and another lodged in McCamon's left shoulder. Mrs. Dexter was quoted as saying that her husband also struck her with the butt end of the gun before he fled.

Mrs. Dexter and McCamon were taken to St. Francis Hospital. Both followed Dexter into the apartment hallway and said he fired

(Please turn to Page 7, Column 1)

HUNT HUSBAND FOR SHOOTING

(Continued from Page 1)

again, the bullet lodging in the stairway leading to the second floor.

Mrs. Dexter said that the rifle used in the shooting was one she had given him for Christmas several years ago. Police believe he may go to the home of Alexander Clinesmith, who lives on a farm near Middleton, Kas., where his children are staying or to a friend in Oregon.

Dexter delivers milk for a local dairy and his wife is employed as a waitress in a local cafe.

know if Oliver felt that way or not, he never said much about it. I was too young to understand that they had problems of their own.

Mother left Daddy and moved to Wichita, Kansas to be near Elva Jean, her sister. Later she got an apartment. My Daddy followed her to Wichita. He got a job at a diary, he ran a milk route.

Daddy went to see her again and tried to get her to go back home with him and be a family again. She said, "NO.' There was another man visiting her in her apartment, while Daddy was trying to talk to her. Daddy could not stand her being with another man. He shot her and the man. Daddy thought he had killed her. He left crying and started to Middletown to see us kids.

The Police called Grandma and Grandpa and told them to hide us kids because Daddy might try to kill us too. I never thought he would hurt us; he just wanted to see us again. He really loved Mom and she had broken his heart. He felt he had lost everything that he had worked for his whole life. While he was driving to see us, his car got hot and he pulled into a field where there was a pond to get water for the car. He was found later by the police. He had got out of the car, put the hood up, went to the pond to get some water, stood there and shot himself. Some neighbor called the police. They came and told Grandma and Grandpa what had happened.

Daddy died 4/29/1942 in Wilson County, Kansas. He was only 42 when he died. We had Daddy's funeral in Fredonia at the Funeral Home. Daddy was buried in Little Sandy Cemetery. Grandma Dexter came down for the funeral. Oliver and I had our picture taken with Grandma Dexter. We didn't get to see Grandma Dexter very often because she lived in Iowa.

The Funeral Director had two dogs. They asked Oliver and me if we wanted to play with the dogs. They were real cute and could do several tricks. The older folks were looking at the caskets and pricing them. Another couple came in to look at the caskets too. I as listening and the man told Grandma a cheaper price on one of them than he had told the other couple. That was the one we picked for Daddy.

Grandma Matilda Dexter lived in Burt, Iowa most of her life. Burt, Iowa was where Daddy grew up too. Daddy's father was Austin Ira Dexter. He was born May 14, 1867 in Charles City, Iowa. He died June 26, 1931 in Houston, Texas. He was 64 when he died. This is their wedding picture.

Estranged Husband Commits Suicide

Body of Russell Dexter Found Northwest of Fredonia; Leaves Suicide Note in Car.

The body of Russell O. Dexter, 41, wanted in a double shooting which occurred in Wichita Wednesday morning, April 29, was found half submerged in a pond two miles northwest of the Farmdale store by John Shafer at 8 o'clock last Thursday evening.

The object of a widespread hunt for the shooting of his estranged wife, Mrs. Lucille Dexter, daughter of Mr. and Mrs. Allen Clinesmith of Middletown, and another man, Robert M. McCamon, 40, in Wichita, Wednesday morning, he apparently had committed suicide some time before his body was found. A warrant had been issued for his arrest and pickup notices were being broadcast from surrounding radio stations for him.

Dexter evidently left Wichita soon after the shooting which occurred in a building at 315 South Water where both Mrs. Dexter and McCamon had apartments. According to Mrs. Dexter her husband entered McCamon's apartment at 2 o'clock in the morning, broke out the door glass and shot his wife in the thigh and left hand and shot McCamon through the left shoulder. He also struck his wife on the head with the stock of the rifle, the Wichita police reported. The sheriff's office in Fredonia was on the look out for him after the police had been informed by Mrs. Dexter that he had told her he was going to the home of his father-in-law, Allen Clinesmith near Middletown, and get his two children, and threatened to harm anyone who might refuse him custody of the children.

His car, a 1939 Plymouth, was discovered Thursday evening at about 6 o'clock and Sheriff C. O. Vice was immediately notified. Neighbors reported seeing the car stuck in a mud hole on a country road eight miles north, one mile west and three quarters mile north of Fredonia. A posse was formed to hunt for Dexter headed by Undersheriff Bill Hayes and assisted by Deputy Sheriff Grover Barb. Sheriff Vice and Lloyd Black went to the Clinesmith home to be on the look out for him.

The body was found at about 8 o'clock half-submerged in a pond about 300 yards east of the car on the old Lon Chapman farm, and the rifle, a single shot 22, was found 25 feet from the body, with the breech open. The bullet had entered his body just under the heart ranging downward and lodging just under the skin in his back. Dr. O. D. Sharp, coroner from Neodesha, was call[illegible] and pro[illegible]unced the death a [illegible] was taken to Fre[illegible]

A suicide note was found in his car in which he left all that he owned to his two children, Oliver and Twylia. He had also recently changed the beneficiaries of his life insurance policy from his wife to his children.

Neighbors reported having heard a car pass the house Wednesday and evidently had gotten stuck in the mud road, but didn't investigate. They saw the car there later but supposed nothing was wrong until hearing of the search being made for a car fitting that description, and immediately notified the sheriff.

Dexter had employment in Wichita as a dairy truck driver.

Private funeral services were held for Russell Dexter Monday at Fredonia.

Dexter was employed for a number of years by the Sinclair-Prairie Oil company at its Kenbro gasoline plant. When that plant was closed a few years ago he was transferred to Texas. The Dexters later returned to Wichita.

FIND SHOOTING SUSPECT DEAD

Russell O. Dexter, 41, who had been the object of a widespread search by police following the shooting of his wife and Robert H. McCamon, was found dead in his motor car about nine miles northwest of Fredonia, Kas., late Thursday.

The sheriff's office at Fredonia notified the Wichita police that Dexter's body had been found and it appeared to be a suicide. Dexter was fatally wounded by a bullet from a small rifle which was found a few feet from the car.

Following the shooting of his wife, Mrs. Lucille Dexter, 31, and Robert H. McCamon, 40, a warrant was issued charging Dexter with assault with a deadly weapon with intent to commit felony.

The shooting occurred at an apartment house at 315 South Wichita when Dexter came to that address armed with a 22 caliber rifle. Police said that Dexter fired the first shots thru the door in McCamon's apartment striking McCamon in the left shoulder and his wife in the hip. They ran into the hall and he fired again hitting her in the left hand and then struck her in the back of the head with the butt of the gun. Both are recovering in St. Francis Hospital.

Dexter then fled. Mrs. Dexter said he had told her he was going to his brother-in-law, Allen Clinesmith, who lives near Middletown, Kas., 15 miles from Fredonia.

Dexter resided at 415 South Laclede in Wichita and was employed as a truck driver for a local dairy.

Austin was a Farmer for years in Charles City, Iowa. Then he went into Real Estate. He listed property stating on the contracts that he would get a percentage for listing and advertising their property. Then he would bill the sellers even if he had not sold the property. Most of the people would go ahead and pay it because they had signed the paper and had not read it. One seller took him to court and Austin lost. Later he was caught doing it again and was sent to Leavenworth, Kansas prison.

Daddy always said his Dad had died when he was 10 years old. Later we found out that he did not die, he just left the family. He came back for a while one time later. Aunt Eunice said, "He only came back long enough to make her Mom pregnant again." That's when she got pregnant with the twins, Eunice and Inez.

He and Matilda divorced in 11/1910. Later he married again in Taft, Texas and they had five children. Matilda never married again. I tried to look up information on Grandpa Dexter one time, but had no luck. The only people that I talked to were young and the women had no idea who their husbands' Grandparents or Great Grandparents were. There were several Dexter's there but no one knew my Grandfather.

This picture is Daddy's mother Matilda Dexter with Oliver and me at Daddy's (Russell Dexter's) funeral. Daddy is buried at the Little Sandy Cemetery in Wilson County, Kansas.

The older kids all got jobs to help with the family. Grandma Matilda Dexter took in laundry and raised a big garden to help feed the family. Austin never helped his family financially in any way. There were seven children in the family.

This picture is Grandma Dexter, born March 26, 1874 in Charles City, Iowa. She died on June 27, 1942, just two months after Daddy died. She was 68 when she died in Burt, Iowa.

My Mother, Lucille was discharged from the hospital. She returned to her apartment and got well. The other man was not hurt very much. I guess Mom called Frank because he came and got her. Mom and Frank Harris got married. They had met and got acquainted when we still lived in Taft, Texas. When they got married they moved to Tishomingo, Oklahoma where Frank's family lived.

Frank and his family were 100% Indian. A couple of years later Oliver and I went to Tishomingo to visit Mother. Frank and Mother lived in a small mobile home behind his Parents house. Frank's Mother treated Mom like a maid. Mother worked hard doing most of the house work for both homes. I felt real sorry for Mom. She was happy to have us visit but hardly had time to be with us. We mostly visited and played with a Neighbor up from their place. My Daddy was always so good to Mother and he showed his love for her in many ways. Even as s small child I could see his love for her.

I guess you can't judge people but she sure had a hard life with Frank and his Mother. Sam was Frank's Father. We liked Sam and he enjoyed being with us. One time we went with Sam to pick watermelons to sell in town. Sam let Oliver drive the team of horses. Sam told Oliver if you accidently hit that big watermelon we can eat it right here in the field. Oliver hit it and we ate the watermelon right there in the field. It was good and real juicy.

Later when we were back at Grandma's we heard that Mother had died. Mother's full name was Alphia Lucille Clinesmith Dexter Harris. Mother was born on 7/6/1910 in Middletown, Kansas in Wilson County. Mother died at age 34, in Ardmore, Oklahoma. She was pregnant and had kidney poisoning.

They had never taken Mom to a Doctor. The baby was dead so the baby was never delivered. Frank did bring her body to us by train to Fredonia. We picked her up at the train depot. She was buried beside Daddy in the Little Sandy Cemetery. Most of the Clinesmiths were buried there. My Great Grandfather George Edward had donated the land to Little Sandy to be a Cemetery.

Oliver was born August 20, 1928 in Madison, Kansas. It was the closest town to Kembro with a hospital. I always looked up to my big brother. He was only one year and eleven months older than me. For that one month I always told him he was only a year older.

1950
Oliver + Dorothy Defter

The year we moved back to Grandma's in Kansas, they were skipping a grade and adding Jr. High to High School in Texas. Oliver was the right age to skip a grade that year. When we started to school in Kansas, he skipped a grade and was a year younger than all his friends.

He married Dorothy Lawson in 1948 in Lawrence, Kansas. He was going to college in Lawrence. Later they had three children, Linda, Russell, and Cindy Jo. Oliver worked for Manor Bakery as a route salesman and later as a Sales Manager. When Manor Bakery stopped selling door to door, he had to find a new job. He applied to Fuller Brush Company and was hired to run a route in Manhatten, Kansas. Later he was promoted to Sales Manager in Dallas, Texas. He spent the rest of his working days as a salesman and Manager for Fuller Brush. Oliver was very lucky and good at playing the stock market. He was investing every penny he could and the market was great.

Daddy's sister, Aunt Trilla married Uncle Herbert Valentine. They had four children Virginia, Gloria, Dewey, and Wanda. Aunt Trilla and Uncle Herbert used to stop in and visit with Lloyd and me when we lived in Claremore, Oklahoma. They would stay overnight on their way to McAllen, Texas as winter Texans.

They lived on a farm and raised Turkeys in Truman, Minnesota. They were big in the Turkey business. They went to conventions and everything about turkeys. They told me that turkeys were the dumbest birds alive. They would bunch up in a pile and smother each other if you weren't careful. Uncle Herbert also liked to hunt. One time he got a big long snake and had it mounted on a board. Just about every time they came to see us, they brought us some kind of wild animals to eat. We had Deer, Elk, and Moose, whatever he could hunt and shoot. I always cooked them but I did not like most of it. I guess I didn't know how to get the wild taste out of the meat.

Virginia Valentine married Bernard Dedrickson. They had two children, Marlene and Barbara. Bernard was a Field Engineer for his Company for 40 Years.

Gloria Valentine married Melvin Schwake. They had three children, Diana, Darla, and Denise. They were both School Teachers. They bought and lived on a farm near Truman, but they did not work on the farm for their living. We were on our vacation and went to Minnesota to see the Dexter branch. Lloyd and I visited with Gloria and Mel at their home. Mel taught me how to play Cribbage. But I haven't played it since. Of course, now I have forgotten how to play.

Herbert [Dewey] Valentine married Mary Teeter. They had one child, Melody. Later they got a divorce. His 2nd marriage was to Sharon Eden. They had three children, Douglas [died as a baby], Debra, and DeAnn. Dewey and Sharon lived and worked on his Dads farm and helped with the turkeys. This was in Truman, Minnesota. His folks left him the farm when they died. Later he sold the farm, and moved into town. After they retired they started going to Tavares, Florida for the winter, it is North of Orlando.

We stopped in to visit them on one of our vacations. They were living in Florida as Snow Birds. Their home was still in Minnesota. Dewey took us for a boat ride down a small Lagoon. We saw a lot of big sea birds nesting in the high tops of trees. There were a lot of alligators beside the lagoon. Dewey said that the first Tarzan movie was filmed in that lagoon. When we got back to their house, there was a big alligator sunbathing on a small lower shelf near the water. I asked Dewey if the alligator could climb up into the yards. He said no, they had not yet anyway.

Dewey took us to Orlando to see the town. We came up behind another car and Dewey just hit the other car. It was dark and you couldn't see very well. They both jumped out of their cars and looked at the cars. Dewey jumped back inside his car and said there was no damage and took off. As far as I know that was the end of it. Dewey was a lot like his and my Uncle Clair.

Jan. 1934

Clair was coming home one time and tried to cross the railroad tracks in front of a train. The train hit him and totaled his car, but Clair was not hurt. He went to a new car dealer and bought a new car, then went on home. He didn't even tell his wife about what happened. Later after the News Paper came out, they started getting phone calls asking how Uncle Clair was feeling. Aunt Lavern would say just fine. After a few phone calls she asked why they were calling about how Clair was feeling. Then he told her and showed her the picture in the paper of the car wreck. It looked read bad. He was so lucky to be all right.

Going back to Aunt Trilla's family, Wanda Valentine married Delfin Wilke. They had five children Lynette, Steven, Gregory, Pamela and Cynthia. Delfin spent most of his life farming in Lewisville, Minnesota. When we went to Minnesota to visit with any of the Family we always stayed overnight with Wanda. Del had died by then. Wanda was my age and therefore was my favorite. Our children were grown by then. Gregory ran the farm for Wanda. He had helped with the farming before Delfin died. He built a new home close to Wanda so they both did have their privacy, but he was close enough to help her with the running of the farm.

When Lloyd and I retired we spent the first winter in Florida. I guess it was just not the best of their winters. The people did not seem friendly. We went to the East coast to Daytona. We saw the car race tracks but there was not a race the day we were there. We went on down to Orlando Beach, We saw several of the sights there, mostly Disney World.

I wanted to see West Palm Beach Florida, where Betty Henley lived. Betty had four girls. Her husband taught them all about water skiing. They skied in computation and her husband did too, but that was in St. Louis. I was very sorry to hear that Betty had cancer. She said her husband was so good to take care of her. When we all lived in St. Louis, her husband was very rude to us, and we were not impressed with him. It was good to know that he had changed toward her. Betty was a fun loving, bridge playing friend.

We went on down to Fort Lauderdale and cut across 75 highway to the west side of Florida. We looked Sarasota over pretty good. Carol's best friend, Debbie in St. Louis had relatives that lived there. They were all with the circus and lived in Sarasota for the winter.

My good friend Joan Tomlinson and her husband, Gene, moved to Clearwater, Florida when he retired. They were on the east side of Florida. They bought a Motel and ran it for about a year. It was a lot of work so they sold it and just retired. Jean developed cancer too. Both of my wonderful friends died of cancer. I miss both of them, we were all good friends. Several years later Gene did marry again. I never met his new wife, but I am glad he found someone else and was happy again. This losing your mate that you love so much is so hard.

The second winter we went to Texas in McAllen, because Aunt Trilla and Uncle Herbert had always invited us down there to see them. When we went to McAllen we found a nice park called Adobe Wells Country Club, we bought a house there. Our house was looking straight at the Club House. We had three walls with windows. The living room was bright with lots of light. We were only about a half of a block to the club house. We were only a cross the street from the Golf Course.

We were so happy and surprised to find that Virginia and Wanda were both sharing a house and still living in McAllen. We went to several events together.

One time we went to the circus; it was a lot of fun. It was the last Circus that I have attended. Another time we went to the fair in Weslaco. We went to the Rodeo. They were both brought up on a farm so they wanted to see the live-stock show. We sit on the benches and judged the bulls. Each of us picked which bull we liked. Now I was brought up on Grandpa's farm and we only had two cows. But I always heard that a good cow had a straight back, so each time I picked a bull with a good straight back. After the judging we heard that each one I picked won the blue ribbon. None of us could believe that I picked the right ones.

Uncle Clair, Daddy's brother, married Aunt Laverne. They had 2 children, Stella [Eden], and Atlee. I always enjoyed going to Uncle Clair's. He would give Oliver and Me a desk of our own. We had a typewriter to write a letter; we had a phone and it was fun to use everything. Uncle Clair and Aunt Lavern ran a Teacher's Service to help Teachers and Schools to get together. Uncle Clair was the head of it but Aunt Lavern probably did the most paperwork. Uncle Clair talked to the people. This is a picture of Uncle Clair and Aunt Lavern on their 50th Wedding Anniversary.

Their daughter was named Stella Iverna Dexter. She went to college and later she was on television, and then in stage productions. While she was acting she changed her name to Dixie Dexter. Later she married Evan Ryl and changed her name again to Eden Ryl. Eden was very successful and started a motivation productions company. She gave motivation talks all around at Company Sales Meetings. Then she started making films to send to her costumers. Her most famous was "Pack your own chute." This referred to jumping out of a plane in a parachute. They had no children. She started her business in New York. Later they moved to California. Then after she retired Uncle Clair and Aunt Lavern moved to California to be near Atlee and his family and Eden. I really missed them in St. Louis. It was like having parents again. They usually came over once a week or at least every two weeks. They would come over on Sunday and eat dinner with us. They were always in a hurry. They didn't want to impose on us.

Don and Pat Webb came over about every Friday night and played Pinochle. One time Uncle Clair & Aunt Lavern, Pat and Don Webb, Lloyd and I had a nice picnic at a park.

Don & Pat Webb - Pinochle

Easter - April 19, 1971

Adams - Dexters & Webbs

Uncle Clair's son Atlee married Roberta Cooke, she went by Bobbie. I have that they only had one boy, his name was Charley. I am not sure what Atlee did for a living. I remember when Atlee was in college he had a motorcycle. He took me for a ride once when we went to visit Uncle Clair.

Oliver and I were at Uncle Clair's and Aunt Lavern's in 1945, when World War II was over! We were upstairs in Uncle Clair's office and everyone was below celebrating. It looked like the whole Army & Navy was there. They were all hugging and kissing all the girls. It was a great party in the street. We all wanted to go and be involved, but Oliver had a cold and Uncle Clair said we could not go because Oliver should not be in the night air, and he would get worse. Finally Uncle Clair could not just watch any longer so he said "I guess it would not hurt him to go and join the crowd. Let's all go! "

Veterans Day was first started as Armistice Day. It was celebrating the end of World War 1 in 1918. It was honoring the Veterans of all of the different branches of the Armed Services. My Daddy was in the Army when they fought in World War 1. Veterans Day has been celebrated every year since. We have had World War one, World War 11, Korean War; actually our men have fought for other countries when we were not even supposed to be in the wars.

Another time we were visiting Uncle Clair and he let one of his office girls, about my age 14, take me to the swimming pool. After we got back from swimming she called me on the phone and we talked about the boys at the pool. I tried not to say anything that would tell the others in the room what we were talking about. She kind of thought the dark haired guy was so cute. I thought the blond guy was the one. After I hung up Uncle Clair played the whole conversation back to me in a room full of his office staff. I just about died from embarrassment. I wonder if he played it back to his office girl. He had a set up to tape conversations in his work so he could remember all that they were looking for in their new employment.

Uncle George Valentine Dexter did not ever get married. I remember one time when we were visiting at Grandma Dexter's In Burt, Iowa, Uncle George took me to town and bought me an Ice Cream cone. He said not to tell Oliver because he only took me. I must have been about 3 or 4, I really felt special.

My Daddy was next in line of the Children. His name was Russell Oliver Dexter. Daddy worked 28 years for the Sinclair Oil Company. He liked to play with us kids. He always had time for us when we all lived together as a family. He was the one that helped me to learn to ride a bicycle. Mom was the one that cooked, made cookies, and made cold drinks for all the kids.

When Daddy was 19 he joined the Army. This article was put in the paper in 1919. "Word was received from Private Russell Dexter, who had recently enlisted and is located at Camp Meade, Maryland, that his division is soon to sail for France."

I really don't remember Aunt Leora. She married Aaga [Andy] Anderson. They moved to California and I cannot remember anything about them. They had 2 children, Ellen and Jane. Jane did a lot of Family tree work too. We consulted several times. I have a lot she sent me that I have been too lazy to get included in my book. I need to get it done for the kids. Maybe when I get this book finished I will get back to working on it. I worked for ten years on Family Tree Book's. I worked on the Adams, the Dexter's, the Clinesmith's and a little on the Bentley's. I kind of burned myself out working on them.

Grandma Dexter had twins after Grandpa Austin Ira Dexter had left the family. She didn't know she was pregnant at the time. She named them, Inez and Eunice. He probably never even knew they had the twins.

Aunt Inez married Clayton Johnson. They had 3 children, Clayton, Larry & Cheryl. Clayton and his wife Pat came to visit us when Claud and I lived in a Mobile home in Laurie, Missouri. We had just sold our big house on the Lake. They had a big deluxe travel bus. It had everything in it; it was all automatic and easy to use. They stayed overnight but stayed in their mobile home. They live in Gautier, Mississippi, very near Biloxi.

Aunt Eunice married Ranny Putz. They had 3 children, Marion [Jack], Gerald [Jerry], and Dennis. Later they adopted Lynette.

Aunt Eunice always wrote to Oliver and me and kept us up to date about the Dexter family. I always enjoyed her letters. None of the other relation wrote to us. She was wonderful to keep writing to us. At least we could remember being a Dexter, thanks to her.

Lloyd and I went up to see them once and Aunt Eunice gave me a newspaper article about Lord Timothy Dexter. She said he was probably a relative somewhere. I read the article and asked Aunt Eunice if she had read the article. She said no. It was about a man that married a rich woman and with her money he built a mansion on an island. He installed statues all around the island. Then he charged tourists money to cross over the bridge to see the island. He was not a relative of ours! At least I could not find any connection.

My Cousin Vera lived in Texas City. Aunt Violet had four children but I really just knew Vera and Opal. We went to visit Ben and Vera and I was

telling her about Grandpa Austin. She worked for a Mortuary and said we would look him up. We discovered that he was buried in Galveston, Texas. She was told that the cemetery that he was buried in was moved. All the other people were moved and they had a record of them, but they had no record of Austin being moved, so he must not have been moved. I guess he is still there under a big Hotel in Galveston. What a nice big monument.

My Grandmother Clinesmith was kind of old fashioned. She thought a man or boy could do no wrong but a girl could not do any thing or people would talk. Later as I grew up my Aunt told me she was always like that. So all the girls were ready to get married and leave her just as soon as they could go. I guess my Mother felt like that because she did marry Daddy pretty young.

Anyway we stayed with our Grandparents and started school. I was in the 5th grade and I went to a one room school in the country. It had one teacher for all 8 grades. Sometimes the older children would help the teacher by giving the younger kids their Spelling words. We had a pot bellied stove to keep the room warm. We all took a sack lunch. We played ball, hop scotch, and my favorite was Handy Over. We threw the ball over the School house, when they caught it, they would run around the house, if they caught someone they had to be on their side.

There were no bathrooms, but there were two little buildings in back of the school. One was for the boys and one for the girls; they each had two holes you could use.

On Sundays they had church in the school. All of the community meetings, dinners, and parties were held in the school. One time some of us girls played church. Thelma was the preacher, I led the singing, Margaret played the piano, and Anna took up the collection, Marjorie was the youngest so she was the audience. The music was horrible, but remember we were just playing.

Sometimes Grandma and I would go pick gooseberries. Some times we would pick blackberries. Either one made good pies. The little yellow sweat bees would eat me up and they would never land on Grandma. Grandma would ask me which job I would rather do. Clean house and help with the cooking or pick berries. I always chose clean house and work in the kitchen.

One time we went to a Community meeting at the school house. It was usually just eating dinner and visiting. When we got home I told Grandma I really liked that pea pie. She said what kind?

I said that pie made with the green peas. She laughed and said that was the Gooseberry pie. The gooseberry pie had a tart taste, but I really liked it.

We had a small mountain not to far from the farm. One day four of us girls decided to go see it and look for Indian arrows heads. We fixed a lunch and planned to be gone the whole day. There was a small open cave up there. We played in there awhile. We couldn't find any good arrow heads but there used to be a lot of them. I guess most of the good ones had been found. We just fooled around, ate our lunch, and talked. We always got home before dark and dinner time.

We lived on a hill at Grandmas. When I walked to grade school, I would cut across the pasture. One time I just about stepped on a big snake. It scared us both. I got a hand full of rocks and tried to kill it but it got away. After that I watched very carefully for snakes.

At the farm we had no electricity so we used Coal oil in lamps to see after dark. I had to check the lamps before dark and make sure there was enough oil for the night. Also when we did breakfast dishes we had to wash the globes on the lamps. Sometimes if the wick was too high, they would get black. Every so often we had to trim the wicks. Grandma always did that. We had four lamps in the house.

Grandpa drove his team of horses hitched to a wagon when he went to get the mail. I went with him. I was playing and jumping on and off the wagon. I missed the wagon and fell on the wheel. Grandpa stopped as soon as he could but I had some scraped skin for awhile.

My Uncle Carl planted a big tomato patch on the farm one year. He told me if I helped with the tomatoes, he would buy me some new school clothes. I would be in High School the next year. I worked with the tomatoes all summer. We put white caps on each plant, later we took them off and hoed all around them. When they were ready to pick, we picked them and went to town. I would knock on the people's doors and ask if they would like to buy some tomatoes. We charged 15 cents a pound. I would tell my Uncle how much they wanted and he would weigh them and tell me what to charge for them. I would give him all the money, and go to the next house. Most of my clothes were from my Aunt Jean. She would get some nail polish on something and then give it to me. I got so I could remodel about anything. I would turn the pleats around and it would look like new. The only problem I had was my Uncle forgot to buy me any clothes. Sometimes it was hard to be happy.

Our cook stove in the kitchen had a well at one end that held water, the heat from the wood fire kept the water hot. When we wanted a bath we would use that hot water in a round wash tub. We usually took our bath in the kitchen because it was warmer in there.

One summer day five of us girls decided to go swimming in the creek. Since I was from town once, I was the only one to have a real bathing suit. The other girls just went in some of their old clothes or under clothes. We were swimming and having a good time and a car came down to cross the river on the low water bridge. The girls all ran toward the trees. I hollered duck down in the water, but no one would listen. I have often wondered what the people in the car did see.

My chores were to gather the eggs every day. I had to feed the chickens. I also had to carry two buckets of water up the hill from the well every morning and every evening so we could cook and drink fresh water. Oliver milked the cow. I thought that looked fun so I wanted to try it. We had a cat that lived in the barn, it would come when someone was milking and we tried to shoot milk in his mouth. Later when Oliver went to college, I had to help milk our cow. I always wanted to try something, and then I would get stuck with the job if I could do it. I don't know why I can't learn to leave well enough alone.

The school had a Pie Supper every year. The girls brought supper in a box. The boys bid on the boxes. They were not supposed to know whose box they were bidding on, but they usually did know. The boy, who bid the highest on the box dinner, sat with the girl and ate the dinner. The Teacher's box usually sold for the most money.

Before we had electricity we bought an ice box. When we went to town, we bought a big chunk of ice. It would keep in the ice box for several days. Grandma would always make some fresh lemonade. That was a nice refreshing drink for the family. It was good to drink cold ice water too.

I remember when we got electricity at the farm. We all stood outside that evening and looked at the big, high light in the yard. You could see the house, the chicken houses, and the smoke house where we kept dried meat, and the milk separator. We used that to separate the cream from the milk. Grandma saved most of the cream to sell when we went to Fredonia.

It was really good to have good light in the house. We could see much better with the electricity. It made doing homework much better. We bought several things that were run on electricity. I think the first thing we bought was a radio. We already had a radio but we had to have a battery for it and the batteries seemed to go dead when you were listening to a really good show. The new one on electricity was much better; it never ran down.

Later when we could afford it, Grandma bought a refrigerator. Then we could have ice all the time. Once in a while we bought ice cream. But most of the time Grandma made the ice cream and we froze it in an ice cream freezer. I used to sit on the freezer while Grandpa turned the handle. They would cover it with an old rug, towels or something. The purpose was for me to hold it still so it wouldn't turn the freezer while they were turning the handle.

Homemade ice cream is so good. We usually just had vanilla but Grandma made chocolate fudge to pour over it. We made the fudge a little runny and when we poured it on the ice cream, it got hard. Yum, it was so good. I still have my ice cream freezer and I still make it sometimes. We heated our water on the stove for hot water to do our laundry.

When we first went to Grandma's, we had a washer that had a handle on the side, and we had to push it back and forth. Then rinse the clothes in clean water and just squeeze or ring the water out by hand. Then we hung the clothes on the line with clothes pins to dry. When we put the clean sheets on the beds, the fresh air smelled so clean and good.

Later we got a real washer that we could hook up to the electricity. It was much easier. We hauled the water up the hill from my Great Grandparents. Grandpa used a big water barrel in the wagon to haul it up to our house. We also caught rain water from the roof of the house for doing laundry. We had a big wooden barrel at the corner of the house and I guess water dripped down the eaves. It was great for washing your hair too.

My Great Granddad, George Edward Clinesmith, was in the grocery store one day and he happened to hear the banker telling the grocery store owner that they were closing the bank for good that evening. He quickly went over and drew all his money out of the bank. This was in 1930. The depression had just started. Due to this, he helped others that had lost everything pay what they owed. He got a deed to their land and said they could pay him back and he would return the deed. Most of them could not pay it back so they lost their farms. Great Granddad would let them stay on the farm for shares, as long as they wanted to stay. After awhile most of them moved on to somewhere else. George's wife was Mary. She always had fresh cookies or donuts in her cookie jar. We kids always liked to go to their home.

Great Granddad, George Edward, gave each of his 5 living children a farm as a wedding gift. The rest of the families made a good living and did well. Grandma & Grandpa were pretty poor. Grandpa never did want to farm. He wanted to be a preacher. He would preach once in a while but never got paid. He rented most of his land and just got a share when the crops were harvested. I guess you have gathered by now, Grandma was the head of our family. Grandma said he was lazy, because after his stroke he didn't do much.

My Uncle Carl, Mom's brother, had a well drilled in the back of our house later for water. This was when I was a senior in high school. We never did have running water in the house. Most everyone had an indoor toilet by now, but we never had one in the house.

I better tell you about our telephone. We had a big one that was attached to the wall. You would speak in the front through a small cone, and to hear, you had a receiver about 2"x5". The phone line was for the whole community. Our ring was one long, one short, and one long.

After Grandpa had his stroke he couldn't do much so he would listen to other people's phone calls. One time two women were talking and said something funny and Grandpa laughed out loud. The women hollered "Allen, get off the phone!" So he got off the phone still laughing.

We could sit around the radio and listen to the programs. Of course there were no televisions yet, so we just had a radio. The most popular show was Amos and Andy. George Burns and Gracie Allen were good too. It was kind of funny; we would all sit around the radio and look at it while we listened to the program or news. Grandpa always sat up for the ten o clock news report.

Once in a while, Mother or Daddy would come by Grandma's to see us. We would all three sleep together in one bed. Mother or Daddy would sleep in the middle and my brother and I would each claim half of them. They probably did not get much sleep. We were both so hungry to see them. I missed them hugging me and loving me. Neither one of them stayed long, just a few days and then leave again. It seemed that Oliver missed the money and living like we used to live. He sometimes got very embarrassed when someone came over to visit with us. I just missed my Parents.

My Grandma was always late. Her favorite trick was to get everyone in the hot car, and then remember to go change her purse or hose. We had instructions to stay in the car, she would be right back. By the time she got back we would all be sweating.

One time my Daddy was going to town and told her he was leaving at 9 A.M. If she was ready she could go with him. She was not ready at 9 A.M. so Daddy left without her. After that, she was always ready for Daddy. No one else, others did not have the guts to leave her.

My Aunt Glenna, Mom's sister, lived at a State Mental Home. She was happy there but my Grandma kept bringing her home every so often. Glenna would be fine if everything went her way, but if it didn't she would throw a fit. One time she was on the school bus, her cousin Opal and a boy were in the seat in front of her. She decided that was not proper, so she hit her cousin over the head with her books. One time she went up in our old rock barn and just sat up there crowing like a rooster. I never did know or realize what that was about. Most of the time she got out of doing any of the work.

I asked my brother to teach me how to dance. I was a freshman in High School. We were dancing in the dining room. Glenna came in and yelled at us, "Dance on Sunday, Dance on Sunday." Each word was getting louder and louder. That scared me so we quit dancing. That's how she would always start her little fits. She would start hollering and each one getting louder until she would throw a fit or until you stopped whatever you were doing that she didn't want you to do. I always thought she just had a bad temper, and was spoiled.

Glenna and I were churning butter. We put the cream in a fruit jar and shook it back and forth until it became butter. After we were through and had butter. Glenna decorated all three of the little bowls of butter. I came in and redecorated one because I had helped so I should get to decorate one. Glenna came in and saw it. She picked it up and threw it on the floor. Life with Glenna was a ball. You never knew what she would do next. I tried to just stay away from her.

Glenna never liked me living at Grandma's. She had always been the baby. Then when I moved to the farm, I was the baby. I really think she resented me for being there at all.

I loved to look at Grandma's china closet. She had lots of pretty dishes. She had several water sets of a pitcher and six glasses. They had one with gold trim and red cherries on them. I asked Grandma one time if I could have that set some day. She said no. She planned to give that set to Oliver. He liked that water set too. Then I asked if I could have the set that was clear with trim of just gold. She said yes because she had not promised that set to any one yet. So for many years, I would always look at my water set with six glasses. It was just clear glass but it was trimmed in gold. But someday it would be mine.

Long after Lloyd and I were married, we went back to the farm to visit. I noticed my water set was gone. I asked Grandma where my water set was. She said she had promised and gave that water set to Richard, my cousin. I went out to the car and cried. She had given my gold water set to Richard. I was really upset. Most of her stuff was antiques.

I went back into the house and looked at the china closet. Aunt Elva Jean had gotten her water set. But mine was gone. The more I thought of it, the madder I got. I picked up a box and packed Oliver's water set in the box. [That was the cherry water set that I had always wanted but of course she said she was giving it to Oliver.] I added a couple of candy dishes that were pink and old. I boxed it all up and took it to our car.

I never told Grandma that I had got Oliver's water set. Several years later, Grandma came to live at our house and she saw the water set in my china closet. She said, "Well, I wondered where that had gone." When Oliver came to our house and saw what used to be his water set he exclaimed, "How did you get my water set?" I told him I just took it and he could not have it back. He had my Mother's diamond rings and he was not going to get the water set. He said OK. He really didn't care anyway.

I still stayed with my grandparents. Oliver went to College in Lawrence, Kansas and became a Jay Hawker. I went on to high school at a little town called Coyville, just 3 miles from Grandma's house. I walked a little more than a mile to catch the school bus.

When I got to the high school I was anxious to get acquainted with the girls there. So I would go up to the girls and say hi, they would turn away and not speak to me. These were the town girls. They would not accept me. Talk about killing my confidence. They were experts. The other country girls did not seem to care. I just did not fit in with the town or country kids.

When you rode the school buses, it was not easy to help with the school activities. I was not used to this kind of treatment and it killed me. I did not like school. I had a few friends but no one special. There was one girl in the 8th grade that I liked, her name was Lois McVey. I was a freshman in the 9th. We were together when it was possible.

I went out with Charles Neuenschwander a few times. His sister, Sue and I got pretty well acquainted. I used to love spelling his name..... Neuenschwander. He was a very nice boy. We went out a few times but Grandma wouldn't always let me go so it didn't last very long. She never thought I needed to go to the ball games at school or the other parties and activities in school.

It was about time for school to start again. I would be a sophomore. We went to a larger town, Fredonia. It was 14 miles away. Grandma went to sell her cream and eggs, I stopped in at that high school. I talked with the Principal, Mr. Lafferty, about me going to high school there. He got a map of the area and asked me where I could meet their school bus. I had to walk up a big hill, but they could turn around up there. They agreed to let me go to the Fredonia

School if I could walk on up the hill. I was happy to agree. I would be the first one to get on the bus, and the last one off the bus every afternoon.

I told Grandma that I was going to go to the Fredonia School to finish high school. She said no. I told her I would not go to Coyville School again, I would quit school first.

Well, school started and I caught the Fredonia School bus. I had to leave earlier and after about three weeks; Grandma asked me why I was later than some of the other kids getting home after school. I told her I was not going to Coyville School, I was going to Fredonia. She finally realized it was Fredonia, or no school at all. I was accepted at the larger school, enjoyed it and I was so glad that I finally won one battle. Grandma and I didn't always get along very well. I guess I have gotten a little stubborn, but sometimes something is real important to me.

One night while I was a sophomore in high school, I went to the movies in Fredonia with a girl friend, Joyce, and her parents. When I came home my Grandfather was in my bed. I asked Grandma where I could sleep. She said to just get in bed with her, so I got in bed.

My Mothers youngest sister, Glenna, was there. Grandma always said she had a sun stroke. She was jealous of me because I was now the baby of the family. Anyway she came in and lay down across Grandma legs, hurting her. Grandma kept telling her to get up and she would not do it. So big, brave Twylia rose up and said, "Glenna get up, you are hurting Grandma." She rose up and wham, she knocked me back down. Just at that time my Brother came in from a date. Grandma called, "Oliver come quickly, Glenna just killed Twylia." He came in and jerked Glenna off the bed.

I don't know what happened to me. I could hear everything but I couldn't move a muscle or speak. Finally I came to and was all right. I guess I fainted but I knew every that was said and done. After that little episode they took Glenna back to the state Hospital in Parsons, Kansas. She was much happier there, she had friends to visit with and talk with.

I found myself unhappy. One day I thought I was nuts to let Grandma get me so upset. I decided to be happy and not let her bother me any more. I decided that she was an adult, I was the child. She had a problem instead of me. I have been happy ever since. I decided to let God take care of me. He has done a good job so far.

One time Aunt Elva Jean and Uncle Ivan came to the farm to visit. Grandma made home made Ice Cream. We were all eating the ice cream and someone said a tornado is coming right to us. Uncle Ivan grabbed the freezer of ice cream and ran to the cellar. We were all in the caller but Grandma. She was hunting her purse. Finally she came just before the tornado got there. The tornado hit the chicken house, the hay wagon, and Grandma said it slid the house over about an inch on the foundation, but it didn't break any windows.

Once in a while I could stay in town with one of my Grandmothers friend, Thelma Muzingo, to go to a school function or a ball game. Thelma would have me set and fix her hair. She also liked for me to baby sit with the worse two boys I had ever met. They loved to lock me out of the house. Sometimes they wouldn't let me back into the house until just before their Mother came home. Needless to say, I didn't like to stay there, but I had no choice.

I took drivers training in High School and got my drivers license. Later I kept asking Grandma if I could drive the car. She always said no, Oliver will drive. One day I picked up the keys and went out to the car and took a ride by myself. When I got home Grandma said," Well I guess you can drive." After that, if Oliver was not home, I drove wherever she wanted to go. Once again, I just had to prove I could do something.

My Uncle Carl & Aunt Oka decided to go back to College for some classes. Uncle Carl was a Band teacher in Fort Scott, Kansas. Aunt Oka was one of his students while she was in high school. Later they got married. They needed me to baby sit for their little boy while she was at her classes. They were going to Lawrence at Kansas University. Oliver was going to college then too. One day Aunt Oka and I were talking about our names. She said she never told anyone her middle name. I asked why? She said they always laugh. I promised I would not laugh. Her name was Oka Ola Hare Clinesmith. I could not help it, I did laugh.

When Aunt Oka was through with her classes, I got a job at the dime store. That was my first real job to get paid a salary. They put me at the candy counter. They said I could eat all I wanted. After the first day I didn't want any more. Then they moved me to the ribbon counter. I worked there until I had to leave to go back to the farm.

Oliver and his friends had a surprise sixteenth birthday party for me in the park in Lawrence. It was mostly Oliver's friends. I didn't care; I enjoyed the party and was happy Oliver thought of it.

The big picture of me on the left was taken when I was graduating from the eighth grade. In the small picture on the lower left, I was about six. I was about 11 in the next one.

In the next frame at lower left, I was a freshman in high school. On the right, I was a graduating senior. In the big picture, I was 18 and recently married.

A friend of Oliver's, Lloyd Adams, came to see him while we were still in Lawrence, Kansas. The next morning I saw Lloyd for the first time as I was coming down the long, winding staircase. I said, "Hello, I heard that you were here." He answered, "If you ever stayed home, I would have seen you last night." I had been out to see a movie with a boyfriend, Richard Nightingale. It was just a few days before I had to go back to the farm in Middletown. Several days passed, and school started. I was a junior in high school. The Adams family lived across the farm on the other side of the Middletown school house.

Lloyd came over and invited me to go to the movie in Fredonia with him. He had blond wavy hair, and was so handsome. We started going together. He had just been discharged from the Army. He fought mostly in Japan and the Philippines in World War II. All the girls were crazy about him. He was 20, four years older than me. Lloyd had been in the Army Tank Division. Lloyd was promoted to First Sergeant of a Battalion when he was 20. In those days, it was unheard of to be a 1st Sergeant at his age. He had his own jeep and a driver. His cousin, Clifton McGaugh, from Neodesha, Kansas went to see him while he was still in Japan. Clifton was in the army at a different base, and couldn't believe that Lloyd had done so well in the Army.

After Lloyd got out of the Army, he went to work at the Fredonia Cement plant. There were hardly any places to work in Fredonia. After about a month of that work he decided that was not the work for him.

He went home and asked Charles, his brother and his Dad, Herbert Adams if either of them wanted to take his job. They both said yes, so Lloyd took them both to work with him and introduced them to his boss and told him they were interested in going to work and he was leaving. They were both hired and worked there until they retired. Charles had been in the Army too. He had got out of the Army several months before Lloyd got out. Charles had served most of his time in Germany.

Lloyd worked for the railroad in Erie, Kansas. He was now a telegrapher and worked for the Santa Fe Railroad.

Lloyd and I continued to go on dates. We broke up several times, because he did not understand that I wanted to go to the school parties & Ball games. He was older and wanted to get serious.

Richard Nightengale sent me a Christmas present by Oliver. I was surprised and sent him a Thank You note for the music box. I had not heard from him and I had not written to him since Lloyd and I had been dating. Lloyd saw the music box and got mad. He told me he had got me a music box for Christmas but he would not give it to me. I never did know what he did with it or if he really bought one.

One time there was a football game at the school and I forgot to ask Grandma if I could go. Some of the kids said they would take me home and ask Grandma if we could go to the game. They were good kids and she didn't have to worry if I was with them. I told them, I didn't think she would let me go. When we got home I asked Grandma if I could go. She said no, I had to do my chores. The kids all pitched in and helped me. Then I asked her if we could go now. She still said no. I asked her why? She said, "Because I said no." They left without me. They couldn't believe it. I never forgot it, I was so embarrassed. I still don't understand why I couldn't go with them. We were not dating, just a group of friends wanting to go to the school game and have a good time.

Lloyd liked to fish and hunt. We went quail hunting one day. I had never gone hunting for anything, let alone a little tiny quail. A bunch of the quail flew up and I raised my gun and shot. One fell down dead. I looked at Lloyd and said, "Did you shoot him? " He said no, he didn't shoot at all and that I had shot it. I quit right then. I didn't want to kill any more.

When I graduated from high school, I asked my Grandma if I could go to college. She said "No, there was no money left for me to go to college." I got a job in town. I planned to stay with my girlfriend Roma at her Aunt's home so we would be chaperoned. I would be working for Mr. Wiggins in his drug store. My Grandma said no; I was needed at the farm to help with the work. She never did let me go to work any place.

She said we had used all of Daddy's insurance money for Oliver's college. My brother had gone to college for two years, and then he got married. I didn't even know Daddy had life insurance. I also didn't know that Grandma was being paid by the government for keeping care of us orphan children. I didn't know any of this until Grandma died and I had to go through all her important papers. Grandma hardly ever bought me new clothes. In fact, I cannot ever remember us going shopping or buying anything. I guess she did buy me a new dress to wear at Daddy's funeral.

Elva Jean did give me some of her clothes that I could remodel and wear to school. I got where I could remodel about anything but I didn't know how to make anything new.

Lloyd and I were still going on dates. I was out of school and I was 17. Lloyd asked me to marry him and he gave me an engagement ring. I accepted and I was so proud of my beautiful engagement ring. I couldn't wait to show it off to everyone.

Grandma just kept planning a bigger and bigger wedding. Lloyd and I were not happy with her plans. She wanted a big wedding at our old farm house. It was not a great setting. Later he came to see me and said he was getting tired of driving back and forth, why didn't we just go ahead and get married. I said okay. Grandma wanted to make it a big wedding at the farm. If we did it her way, she would give me permission. We got the wedding license and the blood tests. So we were ready.

May 30, 1948

My Grandma's family always got together every Memorial day to decorate graves in Buffalo, Kansas. We all got together at Grandma's sister, Aunt Jane's home. While the older relatives were at the cemetery, some of the younger ones went with Lloyd and I to the parsonage to see us get married.

Afterwards, back at my great Aunt's, one of the girls said, "I have just been to a wedding!" Everyone looked at us. Granddad laughed and said, "You put one over on us!" Grandma just frowned and didn't speak. Lloyd and I got married May 30, 1948 in Buffalo, Kansas.

Great Aunt Jane Mayes gave Lloyd and me a fruit bowl. She said, "I get to give you your first Wedding gift." I still have the fruit bowl. It has set on top of my refrigerator for 65 years.

Aunt Violet asked me if we would like to stay overnight at her house. I told her yes, it is really pretty late to start to go to Erie. I always liked Aunt Violet, she was Grandpa's sister.

Aunt Violet lived in the old home place down the hill from Grandma. Aunt Violet had one daughter, Vera, still home. Her children had all gone to Coyville. Aunt Violet had four children but three had already left home. Vera was Lloyd's age and they had gone to school together. After we got married Aunt Violet and Vera moved to Coyville, no one ever lived at the old home place again.

Lloyd and I moved to Erie, Kansas where he was working. He worked for the Santa Fe Railroad. He was a telegrapher. We had a three room apartment on the second floor.

It was fun to go grocery shopping. The first time I went to the store, I bought all kinds of fruit. I bought two of everything in the fruit line. I loved to cook and keep house in our apartment. I was proud that I knew how because several of our friends said they did not know how to do anything when they got married. I guess I need to thank Grandma for that, she did teach me to cook and keep a clean house.

We met three other couples and had wonderful times together. I was the youngest. So they called me baby. It was the Bucks, the Beelers, the Bacons & the Adams. I wonder what ever happened to them. When you keep moving so much it is hard to always keep in touch with your friends. The Beelers had a little red headed girl. She was so cute.

Lloyd would go hunting. He shot a rabbit but I didn't like to eat it. So after that he got squirrels. He would clean them and I would cut them up and fry them for dinner. I would only eat the front legs. There wasn't much meat on that piece. He would eat the rest. We were kind of short on money but much better than at Grandmas. He also went fishing a lot. He would clean the fish and I would fix the fish for dinner. Both his fishing and hunting put meat on the table.

We moved several times. Lloyd changed jobs and went to work at the Missouri Pacific Railroad. We were transferred to Van Buren, Arkansas. He was still a telegrapher with the MOP. That's what Lloyd called it.

One of my best friends is Violet Roberson. We were both living in Van Buren, Arkansas. We met in the Doctors office. We just happened to sit beside each other and started talking. Violet had Bill, her one year old boy in for his yearly check up. I was pregnant with Carol. We talked and I lived fairly close to her. She said, "Come and see me sometime."

I didn't know when sometime was so I didn't go see her. She called me in a couple of weeks and invited us over for Sunday dinner. We went over about 11:30 A.M. The breakfast dishes were still on the table, the living room was a mess with toys and the Sunday paper. I asked her if she meant for us to come that evening. She said no, dinner was about ready. So I gathered up the dirty dishes, cleaned the table and set the table for dinner. Then I picked up the papers and the toys in the living room. Dinner was good. We all ate Billy's Birthday Cake. I cleaned up the table again and we played Pinochle.

We played pinochle quite often with Violet and Theodore. One night Violet said, "Tonight we are going to have a bottle of wine. The men have beer all the time so the wine is ours." Violet and I drank some wine, several times, and then Violet passed out on their bed. I continued playing cards with the men. Theodore kept asking me if I was feeling the wine. I said no, I am just fine. Lloyd said, "I am out of cigarettes. I am going over to the café and buy some." So I decided to go with him. It was nice and cool walking about a block. We walked in the hot café. WOW, it was hot. Lloyd said. "I want a package of Camel Cigarettes." I said, "He wants a package of Camel Cigarettes." He paid for them and we started back to Theodore's. By the time we got back I was ok again. The cool air refreshed me and I felt normal again.

Theodore asked me how I was feeling again. I told him just fine. Lloyd butted in and said, "Don't let her fool you; she repeated everything I said in the Restaurant." That was a night we will remember forever!

One day Violet, Theodore, Lloyd and I decided to go for a nice drive to White Rock Mountain. That was a popular mountain that a lot of people enjoyed just going to see it and how big the mountain really was. We went up and enjoyed the sights. It was getting late so we decided that we better get started back home. We started down the hill. I don't remember which car we had at that time, but as we were going down the mountain, the tie rod broke. We had no control of the car. God was with us... we turned toward the mountain high side. The other side was straight down the mountain, all we could see was the tree tops and they were pretty far down. Lloyd and Theodore got out of the car searching for something to fix it with so we could go on down the mountain. They found an old medal clothes hanger in the trunk of the car. The men straightened the hanger and then wrapped it around the tie rod and it held until we got down the mountain and could stop at a service station.

We were living in Van Bruin, Arkansas. I was expecting my first child. It was time and the pains were getting close. Lloyd was working when it was time for me to go to the hospital. So I called Lloyd and then called Violet. Violet called Theodore's Father. He and his wife came to pick us up and took us to the hospital. He was a nervous wreck taking us. He kept saying hang on we will be there pretty soon. We made it in plenty of time. Lloyd got there before Carol was born. They didn't let the Father go in with the Mother in those days. I wish they could have though; I think they should get to see their baby born.

Carol Jean Adams was born May 7, 1949. She was a beautiful baby. She weighed 6 pounds and 7 ounces. She was born in the Hospital in Fort Smith, Arkansas. Lloyd did not ever get to see any of the six kids born. But he always made it to the hospital before they arrived.

The Doctor would not let me leave the hospital because I didn't have anyone to help me. I told him we did not have any insurance so I needed to go home. Violet said we could go home with her and she would help me. So the Doctor let me go to their home. Carol's basinet had wheels on it, so we played cards and I rocked her with my foot.

The first time we bathed her was exciting. Violet had already had Bill so she was experienced. So she started showing me how to bath her. She was so nervous that watching her made me nervous so I took over the job. It wasn't hard at all; Carol was such a good baby. I always had healthy good babies. I nursed all of them starting out.

One night Violet made a Chocolate cake with white icing. She cut the whole cake in four pieces and gave each of us a fourth. She does not remember that but I will never forget it. We told her we could not eat a whole fourth, she said just eat what you want and leave the rest. We started to play cards and before the night was over we all ate our fourth.

We spent two days with Violet and Theodore. Then we went to our own apartment. We were upstairs on the second floor. We had one bedroom, kitchen, living area, and bath room.

When Carol was two weeks old we went to a movie. She slept most of the time, and then she woke up with a dirty diaper. I walked home, only 2 blocks away, changed her diaper and ran back to the movie. Remember I was only 18. I had a lot of energy then. We only had cloth diapers then. We had to wash the diapers and rinse them at least two times, hang them on a clothes line and when they were dry, bring them in the house and fold them and put them away. We did not have disposable diapers yet.

One day I made a beautiful two layer Chocolate cake with fluffy white icing. I put it in the middle of the table. Then we went to town for a little while. When we came back home the cake was full of those little piss ants. We were on the second floor. They crawled up the side of the building, into the kitchen, over to the cake and had a field day eating the cake. It did not look as good when Lloyd got rid of the cake.

When Carol was about a month old, she woke up in the middle of the night to nurse. While I was feeding her I noticed something round and white on the soft spot of her head. I woke Lloyd up and he casually lit a cigarette and started smoking. Then he held the hot end of the cigarette close to the tick and it backed out of her head. Then he killed it. It was full of blood. He had been hunting and had brought the tick back on his clothes.

Van Buren, Arkansas was built kind of different. There were a lot of triangles built in the roads. It was on the side of a large hill and there was not much level ground. Lloyd was a telegrapher while we lived there. We lived pretty close to the railroad. About four blocks, Roberson's lived about two blocks from the railroad. The Roberson's and we stayed good friends for many years. Violet and I are still good friends and go on trips together.

Carol was two when we were transferred to Claremore, Oklahoma. We rented a duplex. We had a bedroom, Living room, Kitchen and Bath. Shorty and Hazel lived in the other half. They were a nice older couple.

One Sunday Bill & Pat Grace, Lloyd and I were just ridding around. Bill asked if we had ever been in Eureka Springs, Arkansas. We said no. So we took out for Eureka Springs. Pat had a diaper bag for Gordon, and one bottle of milk. The rest of us had nothing to stay over night. We checked in at a Motel and the men went to find milk. Pat washed some diapers. Later we went out to dinner, and then came back to the Motel. Carol really thought she was a big girl. Gordon was still just a baby. We shared the Motel. We were almost asleep and Bill said, "Pat stop that, we are not by ourselves." A little later he said, "Pat, not tonight!" This was Bill's idea of a joke on us. Just in fun.....

The next morning when we woke up I looked out the back window. Down, down, there was nothing but sky to see. The motel was built on stilts. The front was pretty green grass but the back was sky. It was a very interesting town. We rode around the town and we saw the Spring Well in Eureka Springs. The whole town was built on and between mountains. Lots of the buildings were built on stilts. It was a fun day. We had to get back home, the men both worked on Monday.

Now I found that I was pregnant with my second baby. I called Grandma and asked if she could come and stay with Carol and Lloyd when it was time for me to go to the hospital to have our baby. She said, "Yes, I would be glad to come and to take care of Carol and help Lloyd."

The baby was just about due so Lloyd went to get Grandma. I went to the hospital shortly after Grandma came, the baby was coming. The hospital was dismissing another Mother and baby so they had me wait until they were through. I was standing by the drapes crying. Lloyd came up to me and asked what was the matter. I told him the baby was coming.

He took my arm and said come on. We by passed the front desk and Lloyd took me on down the hall looking for a nurse. One walked by and Lloyd took her arm and told her to check me. She did and said "Oh my, the baby is coming!" She took me in a room and called the Doctor. They delivered the baby and put me in a room. It only took a half hour.

We named our little boy James Allen Adams. I had a little trouble after Jimmy was born. I kept calling for the nurse to check me and she kept saying I was all right. It just did not feel right, so about the third time, I saw a different nurse and called her to check me. She asked if I could wiggle my fingers, I could not. She asked me to wiggle my toes. I could only wiggle the toes on one foot. She called the Doctor again. I was hemorrhaging. Lloyd had left after the baby was born to go eat and when he came back, I had the Doctor and two nurses around me. He just about passed out. One of the nurses helped him to a chair.

Jimmy was a big healthy baby. He weighed 9 lbs. He was born November 26, 1951. I went home when Jimmy was 3 days old, but the Doctor said to stay in bed several more days until I got some strength back.

When I got home Grandma was gone. She had gone to her sisters to visit in Skiatook, Oklahoma. She had left to visit her sister when I went to the hospital. She was gone the whole time I was in the Hospital. Lloyd had to take Carol to friend when he had to go to work. She was still at Pat Graces' when I got home with Jimmy.

Lloyd was by himself. Lloyd tried to fix something for supper. He put tomatoes in the pressure cooker, when the steam had built up he noticed that the handles were not together. He squeezed them together and it exploded over Lloyd and the whole kitchen. I jumped out of bed and ran into the kitchen and Lloyd told me to get back in bed. I wouldn't go until he said he would go next door and Hazel would help him.

He had just returned to our apartment when Grandma came home. I was so mad I screamed at her because she was not here taking care of Carol, and helping like she was supposed to be. Grandma's sister from Skiatook had brought her home after her 3 day visit. I told Grandma it was the first time I had ever asked for her help and we couldn't trust her when we needed her. She was supposed to take care of Carol and help Lloyd. Instead she left and spent the whole three days with her sister. She could just go back with them if we couldn't depend on her help. She did stay and later Lloyd took her home. It was one of the few times she was nice to me. She knew she was wrong. I don't think Lloyd ever cooked again.

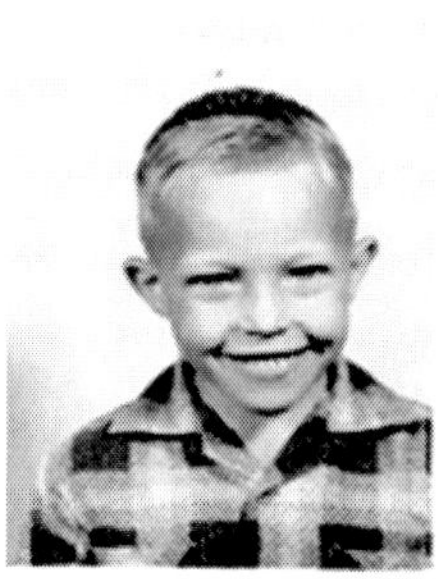

SCHOOL DAYS
1958-59

These photos are Jim age 7, his graduation from Pattonville High School in 1969, and his wedding.

Jim married Mary Busman May 28, 1977. They met while working in a restaurant. Jim was a waiter and Mary was a hostess. Jim went to Columbia, Missouri to College. Mary followed him there. Mary had already graduated from college. I don't remember where. She went somewhere in Europe.

One of Mary's ancestors started the Bus Fuse Company. Thomas Jefferson invented the Fuse and went into business with a friend. They named the business after the friend who was a Busman.The bus fuse went into a car to start the lights and I don't know what else. Mary's family kept the business going until the two brothers retired and then sold the business.

Our Jim and one of Mary's brothers started their own company in the computer business. Mary's brother ran the business end and Jim ran the sales. The business grew and did great. This picture is by their house in St. Louis.

Jim and Mary only had one boy, they called him Jimmy. Later after Jim died of Cancer, Jimmy changed his name to Jim.

Shorty and Hazel liked to watch Television but they did not have one. They came over every Saturday night to watch boxing if we were going to be home.

Lloyd had surprised me with the Television after I had gone to his folks for a short visit when we were expecting Carol. He had told everyone about the big surprise for me when I got home. I had really hoped the big surprise was a washing machine. We enjoyed the television but I had to go to the laundry place to do our laundry. After Carol was born I usually had to go at night so Lloyd could watch the baby. Carol was growing up and is a pretty girl. Carol will be 2 ½ when the new baby arrives.

While Lloyd was working as the Depot Agent in Claremore, Nat King Cole's group came to travel on the train. They had put on a big show in Tulsa. Nat asked Lloyd if they could use both sides of the depot for his group. It was a large group so Lloyd said yes; they could use the white side too. In those days the railroads always had two sides. One was for the white people and one was for the black people.

We were living in Claremore and my Daddy's sister and her husband, Aunt Trilla and Uncle Herbert Valentine, were on their way to McAllen, TX. We were a good place to stop in and break the trip. It was fun to have them. They were called Winter Texans from Minnesota. They always invited us down to visit them but Lloyd had to work, and we just never could go.

I liked Claremore; it was a nice town and we had several railroad friends there. The Will Rogers Memorial and the Davis Gun Collection was there. The Will Rogers Memorial was so interesting. He was a Newspaper man that traveled everywhere and had a knack of writing the news in funny comments. The Gun collection was quite unique. They had guns of all kind. They had a little pistol that would really shoot. They had a little rifle that they could shoot. They had all sizes. The men were really interested in seeing the guns. We had lots of company while we lived there, and we took all of them to see both. At Christmas, I think it was one of the prettiest decorated small towns that I had ever seen.

We were living in Claremore while they were building the turnpike between Missouri and Oklahoma. It was explained to all of us in the News Paper that there would be a charge on the road until it was finished, then it would be a free road. So far there has always been a charge and that was 70 years ago.

Lloyd was transferred to Nowata, Oklahoma. Carol started first grade in Nowata. I had a little iron baby bed that I had used with Carol and Jimmy. We had a friend that had just had a baby and asked if they could borrow the baby bed. It had been in our Family for many years. I loaned them the little iron bed. I told them that I wanted to keep it so my daughter could use it as a doll bed later. One night they moved away and took it with them. I never heard from them again. I was really upset they had stolen our antique iron baby bed.

Two years later, January 31, 1955, Jerry, our 2nd boy was born in Nowata, Oklahoma. I started nursing Jerry as I had such good babies with Carol and Jimmy. However, I had trouble nursing him; I guess I didn't have enough milk. This started when he was about 3 months old. The Doctor said just go ahead and put him on the bottle. I tried but after my nipple, the bottle was so hard. I boiled the nipples trying to soften them; he still would not take the bottle. So finally I would hold a glass for him and he would drink from the glass. This worked for us. But later it became clear to me that he didn't get enough sucking when he was a little baby. He developed a habit of making a sucking noise. He finally out grew that but it took several years. Jerry was a good baby though and a sweet baby boy.

Jerry met Mary Ryan in the restaurant and bar while he was working in Balaban's. They started dating and decided to get married. Jerry and Mary went to Hawaii to get married. This is their wedding picture.

They had a big reception for their family and friends on a riverboat on the Mississippi river.

They came back to Creve Coeur and bought a house. Later they had one little girl that they named Melissa. A couple of years went by and Mary decided that she wanted to be a nurse. They were thinking how they could manage that with a small child. Jerry was a bartender at that time. They decided he could work at night and Mary went to nurse's training in the day time. Jerry asked me if I thought that would work. I said yes, but when would you be together? They said it would only be for one year.

It did work, Jerry worked at night, I have often wondered if Jerry got any sleep. Mary got her Nurse degree. They spent a whole year not seeing each other very much. Then they got a divorce. Neither one of them has remarried. Mary did move in with a doctor several years ago.

Jerry + Melissa 2008

Melissa split her time with both of her parents. After she was grown she shared her Dad's house with other college friends. Jerry had moved and bought a two story town house.

Lloyd joined the Elks Lodge in Nowata. One day he came home and said they were going to have a big party and dance. He said if I wanted to go I would have to find an older woman to baby sit. This was the first baby sitter that Lloyd agreed we could have after twelve years. So I was really excited and happy to get out with no children. He always said, they were our kids and we would raise them. Meaning me! He was always working or traveling someplace.

I was so excited. At the party everyone thought I was drinking because I was having so much fun. I was not drinking anything but Coke. We had some friends Charles and Roberta Meeker. They were both flirts. I had just finished dancing a dance with someone and as we were walking back to our table, Lloyd was walking right in front of me. Lloyd had his arm still around Roberta, hugging her. It made me so mad; I knuckled him on his hand hard. When we got to the table he asked me what that was for. I said the music and the dance was over. Now I realized why he wanted me to get a baby sitter and go to the dance. That was one thing he couldn't go to without me.

A couple of years later, Charles Meeker ran away with their neighbor lady, and then Roberta and the neighbor man got together and married. They got both houses and all the kids. I told Lloyd that could have been us that they broke up.

I vowed then that I would never get a divorce. I told Lloyd that after we had been married several years. I told him there was only one way we would be separated and that was by death. We were lucky, we had a good marriage & Lloyd was a good man.

Lloyd went to the Veterans of Foreign Wars every Saturday night. He loved to play Poker on Saturday night. I stayed home and raised our kids. I was lucky again by always having a car. I would have to always take the kids but at least we had the transportation. We went to the park and the kids would play. We went to the grocery store. Sometimes just rode around looking at the country.

I got better acquainted with Roberta and she usually did not have any transportation. I would call her if I was going to the grocery store. She and her boys would ride with me. She would never make her boys mind. They would jump around in our car; they would jump on my beds if they were at our house. I hated to tell them not to, I kept thinking their Mother would tell them to behave but she never did make them stop.

One day Roberta called me and said they had the car today. Would we like to go with them to the store? I said sure. We started to get into their car and David, the oldest boy said, "We are in our car today, we cannot play in the car, we have to sit still and take care of our car." I could just hear their Mother or Dad telling them they had to take care of their car. From then on, I treated them just like I would treat my own kids. She never said a word to me about my rules. I learned from Roberta to take care of my own stuff, nobody else would if I didn't.

Lloyd was still working as the Telegrapher and Depot Agent. While there, the Railroad started cutting off jobs. The first thing we knew, Lloyd was back on the extra board or without a job. Now we had 3 children.

My Brother, Oliver, was working for the Manor Bakery as a route Sales Manager. Lloyd asked him if he thought he could get a job with Manor. Oliver said yes but don't tell them they were brothers in law, unless he did a good job. Lloyd went to Kansas City and got a job with them. He started working as a route man in Independence, Kansas. Manor Bakery had their Bakery in Kansas City. They also delivered Bread and other pastries door to door. Lloyd became Sales Manager for Manor. He would bring a Manor fruit cake or an applesauce cake home for me to cut up in small bite pieces. He would pass them out to customers. He sold a lot of the cakes after the customers had a taste of them. The kids and I ate the scraps, both cakes were really good.

While in Independence, Dexter, our 4th child, another boy, was born. He was born 4/10/1957. Marjorie came over to stay with the other kids while I was in the hospital. Marjorie was Lloyd's sister. We walked across the street to the hospital. My pains were pretty close together. They said my Doctor was tied up in surgery and it would be about an hour before he would be through.

They put me in my room. My pains stopped. A little time later they brought my lunch. It was Ham and candied sweet potatoes. I rolled over and took one bite. I had one long hard pain; the Doctor was coming down the hall with his hands up in the air. They took me into the delivery room and he delivered Dexter right away. It had been exactly one hour. That's what I call timing it just right. The nurse came in to get the tray, I said leave it here, I am hungry, so I finished eating my lunch. We appreciated Marjorie taking care of my kids while I was in the Hospital. I took care of Marjorie when she came home from the hospital when Donna was born. I was giving Donna a bath the next morning and I noticed Donna had a birth mark on her leg. I showed the mark to Marjorie and she said "Oh no!" It wasn't that bad, it was hardy even noticed.

Grandma and Grandpa were living part time in Fredonia at Great Aunt Bell's house. Aunt Bell had given the house to Grandma because we kept care of her at the farm when she was sick until she died. I had helped with her, but I sure did not like doing it. She was so old.

Anyway, we were all going to be at Aunt Bell's house for Thanksgiving. Aunt Bell's house was in Fredonia, Kansas. We were living in Independence, Kansas now. Most of the family was already there when we got there. Elva Jean & Ivan March, Uncle Carl, Glenna, Patty and Family, Glenna's daughter, & Grandma. I said Hello to all the men and Glenna. They were all sitting in the living room. Then I went on to the Kitchen to help cook. After awhile Glenna yelled "Twylia is stuck up". "Twylia thinks she is better than we are!" Each time was a little louder, just like her usual progress for a fit.

Then dinner was ready for us to eat. Glenna hollered at me again. I told my Family we were leaving. I didn't have to put up with Glenna's fits toward me anymore. So we gathered up our Family and left.

Aunt Jean and Grandma both said, "Don't go, dinner is ready. Glenna will be good." We left. We couldn't find any place to eat. Everything was closed for Thanksgiving. We found a filling station that had cold cuts and chips. We bought some crackers, baloney and cheese, and went to a park to eat. It was cold. Everyone was miserable. After that, Glenna never hollered at me again or gave me any more trouble.

Grandma gave me some of her old big money. It was old money bigger than our dollar bills. Jim wanted my favorite which had an Indian in red in the middle of it. I gave Jim 4 of the big dollars one was the red Indian, I gave Jerry 3, and Dexter 3. I gave Oliver 5 of them. I didn't have any left. When Oliver died years later, Cindy Jo asked me what I would like to have of Oliver's. I told her the big money that I had given to him. Oliver had put the bills in a clear picture frame. She did give it to me. I have it on my computer desk right now. I think of Oliver almost every day when I see them. Years later Cindy and Linda Dexter came over to see me. Linda asked if when I died, I could leave them the big bills that I had given to Oliver. I said yes, I wouldn't need them any longer.

While we were still living in Independence, Lloyd was hunting one day and found a new baby squirrel. It didn't even have his eyes open yet. We kept it and it stayed in the house. He loved to sit on the top of the couch; he was brown and matched the couch. When company came, the squirrel would jump down and startle the people. He was a good pet until one day he got out and was gone.

Bob and Vera McVey, my cousins from Neodesha, came to visit us. I told Vera we were going to the park, and have a picnic; this was before they came to our house.. When they came Vicky was dressed so cute like she was going to church. Needless to say, she got dirty playing.

I have always felt close to Vera and her Family and have enjoyed being with them. I will never forget one time we were at Vera's when the still lived in Neodesha, Kansas. She made some homemade noodles. I told her to look here and I would take her picture. She looked at me and dropped a hand partly full of noodles. We both laughed and cleaned up the mess. I have always made homemade noodles for my family too. They are so good.

We weren't in Independence very long until Lloyd was promoted to a route in Olathe, Kansas. Lloyd found us a house about 2 miles out in the country. It had a beautiful 2 story house with a winding stairway. The garage was in back of the house with a long drive way.

It was kind of like the house in "Gone with the Wind." It was great living there while the weather was good. I took Carol and Jimmy to school every morning. Dexter and Jerry were still home and we went roller skating every Wednesday morning. I got the boys some plastic skates and we all skated. I loved to skate and dance to "When the Saints go Marching In."

Lloyd was still working in Topeka, Kansas. One morning in Olatha, we had about 5 inches of snow. We were snowed in. I could not take the kids to school. I started shoveling the snow hoping I could get the car out because we were getting low on food. I was used to going to the store about every other day. After about 3 days I was getting desperate. I had worn out several pairs of gloves trying to shovel the car enough to get out. I still could not get the car out. What could I do? We were out of food; the kids were too young to take out. We lived about two miles from town.

I noticed a farmer feeding his cows on his tractor. I quickly wrote a list and got some money and went over his fence to talk to the farmer. I asked if he would go to the store for me I had four kids and had run out of food. He agreed to get my groceries. He wasn't gone long; I thanked him over and over. I appreciated it so much. We lasted a couple of more days and the snow melted.

Just as soon as the snow melted I took the kids back to school and went to town looking for a house in town. I found one, rented it, called some moving men, called Lloyd and told him we didn't live there anymore. The very next day we moved to town.

The moving men could not believe how quickly I got settled. I was all unpacked and moved in while the men were hooking up the washer and dryer. I made them some coffee and they set down and had a cup of coffee before they left. Some of my memories of Olathe were not that good. I was so worried about the kids. I don't think Lloyd ever understood how scared I was being snowed in and couldn't get out to buy food for the kids.

One time some of my friends and I were talking about raising our kids. We got on the subject of bathroom training. One of the girls said it was so hard to train her son. I spoke up and told them that my son Dexter trained himself. He just got in the habit of going when one of the other boys went. I didn't even realize when he was trained.

We had our milk delivered to our house. The route man asked if we were relation to the Adams just 2 blocks away. I said no. Later we went home to visit Lloyd's parents. They asked Lloyd if we had gone to see Kenny his cousin in Olathe. We said no, we didn't know they lived in Olathe. A few days later, we went to see them and they were in the process of moving to the north part of Kansas City.

There was a school for the deaf in Olathe. Our next door neighbors were one of 8 children. Four of them were deaf. One day I noticed their little red headed girl and Dexter was playing outside. Dexter was probably about 4. Dexter was talking with his hands. He had picked up the deaf sign language from the little girl. He quickly forgot it when we moved again.

Dexter went to Warrensburg, Missouri College. He graduated with a degree in Business. Dexter and Susan met in College where they both were going to school. Susan taught school one year. They got married in 1979 in Susan's parent's church.

They were married for a couple of years and Susan went to the Doctor. She could not seem to get pregnant. They talked it over and decided to adopt a baby. They adopted Aaron Andrew Adams, on June 6, 1988, a sweet baby boy. In a couple of years they wanted another baby.

This time they tried having Dexter donate the seed and the Doctor inserted it. It took the second time and they had a little girl named Amber on March 17, 1991.

Growing up, my brother and I always played games. He loved Monopoly. I don't think he ever lost a game. One time while dating Lloyd, I had lost all my money and property to Oliver, so I became the banker. Lloyd also kept loosing so I slipped him money. Oliver ended up with all the banks money and ours. I just thought of that because I raised all my children playing all kinds of games. The only thing Lloyd would play was Poker. So we all played poker with him when he was home and could play.

A couple of girls in Carol's school were walking home from school one day and it was bad weather. One of the girls was struck by lightening. It killed her. I had never thought of such a thing happening. The other girl was not hurt at all.

We had bought a water skiing boat while we were living in Olathe. It was a white 16 foot Cosby. It had everything on it, plus two automatic reels for water skiing. We bought it on my Birthday. Lloyd said it was my present. That was the last time he remembered that it was mine.

Lloyd was promoted to Sales Manager of Manor Bakery at Topeka, Kansas. We built our first new house. It was a 2 story raised ranch. The living quarters were up stairs with the double garage and recreation room and ½ bath down stairs. The front of the house was the double garage and the Recreation room on the street.

My stove was old and I had to prop the door closed with a chair. After living there for several months, I told Lloyd I had to buy a new stove. He finally said go ahead and buy one. I went to town and fell in love with a stove. It had 2 ovens on the top, a pull out drawer for the stove burners with a cutting board in front. The storage for the pots and pans was in the bottom of the stove. I bought it. They delivered it the next day. Lloyd came home and said "Good God Twylia, the Governor couldn't afford one like that." I loved that stove for many years.

Lloyd was the Sales Manager. Jim Hamilton, Marshall Lett, and Bob Armstrong were assistant Sales Managers. Jim's wife was Beverly, Marshall's wife was Elizabeth, and Bob's wife was Flo. All three of the wives and I became good friends. Lloyd would ask me to set up all the business parties, so the other girls would help me.

We had a lot of company. Some of the guys played music and we had some good parties at our house. Marshall could not hear a song without wanting to sing. Marshall and Beth had four boys about the same ages as our kids.

One time we were planning a business party and as we were going to town, I asked the girls where they wanted me to park. They told me where and I pulled in to park just where they told me. After that it was a game we played to see if I could park where they told me.

Someone at one of the parties sat on my stairs smoking and burned a hole in my new carpet. After that I announced that no one can sit on or go up on the stairs. We had a half bath down stairs.

July 6, 2002 · Beth + Marshall Lett

The music was played in the Recreation room. One time Beverly and Jim stayed after a party and helped us clean up. They couldn't believe how much work it was to clean up after one of the parties. At the next party they told everyone else to help and it would not take so long.

I decided to terrace the back yard so the kids could have a better place to play. I talked the builder into tearing down a rock tower that was not safe so we could use the blocks to build a wall.

The worker that was grading the ground was just making the back yard a hill. I wanted a patio on the top level and the lower level for the kids to have a place to play. He graded the ground just like I asked him. I was at the end of the line of houses, so I helped all the other neighbors to build their wall. We all worked together. The only problem was when they got their yards done they quit. They had used most of the good complete blocks, and most of mine were broken. I did mine by myself and got so mad at the others for not helping me. Lloyd didn't even help me. I could really throw those big cement blocks while building the wall. You get extra energy when you are upset. It was all my idea and no one else seemed to even know it. As God says, "That too will pass." I did like our yard when it was finished. It made a better place for the kids to play.

I was Carol's Girl Scout leader while we lived in Topeka. I had 16 girls every week and it was fun. I had 2 girls each week watch Jerry and Dexter to earn their badges. I enjoyed working with the girls. I ended up being the Neighborhood chairman of the Leaders of the girl's troops. At the first Neighborhood meeting, very few of the leaders were on time. I explained to them, I would repeat this time but the next time they were late I would not. By the third meeting everyone was on time.

When I had a Birthday Party with only 4 boys, I would be totally worn out. So I was just room Mother for the boys while they were in School.

Lloyd was having a big sales meeting in Topeka and he invited all of his men to join us at the lake whenever they could. We always went on Sunday afternoon at Pier 5. I think they all came almost every Sunday. The only way I could ever water ski was when Lloyd was out pulling some one else. I would tell the men I was next. The other women never even got to be in the boat. I don't think any one else ever bought gas or if they tore up a life jacket, no one ever offered to buy a new one. Lloyd was the boss, so we were rich. They thought!

We always had a boat while we were raising the kids and we were always in or near water. We taught all the kids to swim and water ski. We enjoyed boating, skiing, fishing, or just to be on a picnic.

While the men were boating, the ladies and children gathered at the picnic tables and visited. One day I asked if any of them played Bridge. They all said no. I couldn't believe it, surely someone could play. I wanted to learn. Finally one girl said she had taken one lesson. I asked what she learned at her lesson. She told me each week and that is how I learned to play Bridge. My neighbor lady played so I asked her if I could play with her some day. But be sure and tell the others I am a brand new player and have never played a real game.

About a week later she called and invited me to come to her house to play. I was thrilled and reminded her I had not ever played. I walked in her door and she was having a 3 table bridge party. I just about died. She said if I needed help to just go ask a dummy at another table. She put a bridge table cloth on my table. I could read some of the things I had learned. One hand my partner and I bid a slam, it was there, I could see it. I had to play the hand. Then I lost transportation to the dummy. I could have cried, but I sure learned to watch for transportation.

Lloyd said when we got moved to our home in Topeka, that at least we would never have to worry about a tornado. Burnett's mound was just south of us a couple of blocks. He said if a tornado came by the Burnett mound would make it jump right over us.

Violet and Theodore came to visit with us in Topeka, Kansas. They flew up in their small plane. We took them boat riding, swimming and water skiing. We had a great time. I was driving the boat, zig sagging around trying to get a big loud scream from them.

The next day Theodore asked me if I would like to go for a short airplane ride. I said yes, I had never been in a little two passenger plane before. When we got up in the air

Theodore asked me, "Were you trying to scare me in the boat yesterday?" I said NO, Theodore. Then he said you don't have to worry, when you are in an airplane you don't play around. They lived in Okmulgee, Oklahoma then. Theodore was a professional glass cutter. I never knew anyone with that occupation before Theodore.

Lloyd was promoted and we moved to Mexico, Missouri. He was sales manager for all of Missouri. We sold our home in Topeka when he had to move. A couple of months later a Tornado did come by our house in Topeka and took the top floor away. The new buyers had good Insurance and they replaced the top floor, they fixed everything and insurance paid off our Veterans loan. We were lucky and blessed again.

We moved into an older established neighborhood in Mexico. It was lovely and the Families had lived there for years. They were real friendly out doors but not one invited me in their homes. So I was very lonely. As usual, Lloyd moved us in and went to work out of town. I had workmen in to fix something every day for a while. Then one evening Lloyd called and I told him I was so lonely. All the repair work was done; no one else ever came to see me. Lloyd was only home on week ends.

That is when I called the bowling alley and asked if they had room for me to bowl in a league. I joined a ladies league. Then I began to get acquainted with friends. Some played bridge so I joined a bridge group.

Lloyd brought a little dog home one day. It was a little Chihuahua. Lloyd said we could call him Clyde or Cecil. We decided he would be Clyde.

A day or two later I went to play Bridge. I was telling them about our new dog. I told them Lloyd gave us a choice of two stupid names and we chose Clyde. As usual, I couldn't think of the other name. Her husband came home and she introduced her husband. His name was Cecil. For once I was glad of my bad memory.

Polly was born in Mexico, Missouri. She was born December 20, 1963. She was born 7 years after Dexter. She was a cute blond baby girl. Everyone thought she was the cutest baby ever born.

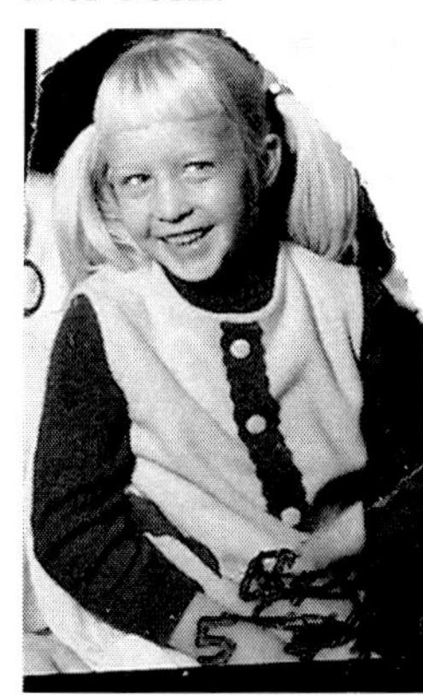

The whole family spoiled her. Jim actually took care of her. He was fascinated with her. He even took her on one of his dates when she was two or three. She enjoyed telling friends that she was born in Mexico. She didn't add Mexico, Missouri.

The day we came home from the hospital after Polly was born; we were watching television in the family room in the basement. Dexter came down the stairs, slipped and fell down two steps. He seemed OK. We watched TV awhile, and then Dexter woke up from a nap and started talking baby talk. He was 7 years old. I couldn't take him to the hospital so Lloyd had to take him. He had a brain concussion.

Dexter had to take medicine the rest of his childhood or he would have times when he couldn't stand to have any clothes on and he wouldn't know what he was doing. We never could find out just what the problem was but he got better when he grew up and stopped taking the medicine.

We vacationed several times in Gravois Mills. It was a great place for us to boat, swim, & play. Lloyd and Polly liked to fish. One day Lloyd caught a 5 lb. catfish. He said now we can have fish for dinner. Just a little later Polly caught a 5 lb fish.

Everyone ran to get their cameras to take a picture of her and her fish. Lloyd said, "I don't get it, I catch a big fish and nobody cares; Polly catches one and everyone goes wild!" I reminded him that she was12 and he was a little older.

Jeffrey was fishing with Lloyd on another day. Jeff caught a fish. It was a little fish but Jeffrey was so proud of catching it.

With what Lloyd had caught and Jeff had caught, we had fish for dinner.

We started going to Branson, Missouri on our vacations. We stayed at Harry's resort that was close to Silver Dollar City. We bought this 16 ft Cosby boat and had lots of fun on vacations with it. The kids used to line up for their turn to ride and waterski.

One time Lloyd was going to water ski. When the boat took off, he was sitting on a nail on the dock that tore his swimsuit off! Just as he realized what happened, he dropped the rope and sunk into the water. He wore a towel for the rest of the day!

Lloyd caught a big fish and Jim Hamilton wanted to show us how big it was by comparing to a 5th of V.O.! Then they drank it.

After a couple of days with swimming, horseshoes, and fishing, the kids all decided to go to Silver Dollar City. It was a fun day with lots of things to see. They had old time stuff to see, like how you made candles, cutting wood, blowing glass, and many other things to learn. They had all the rides, food, and entertainment shows. It was a full day but we all had a great time.

We enjoyed going to the Lake of the Ozarks for vacations. We went to the same place at Mill Creek Resort in Gravois, Missouri. Oliver and his family came and spent a week with us.We shared the work, cooking, buying groceries, by that I mean Dorothy and I. I think everyone enjoyed that vacation. The kids enjoyed swimming and water skiing the most. They became a little better acquainted with each other too.

Lloyd and I were fishing in a covered dock. It was so cold. I caught a Dog Fish. I was so excited. I had never seen a Dog Fish before. A quick glimpse showed me a weird fish with four legs, a head like a fish and a tail. A man standing near me said he's take it off the hook for me. He did and threw it back in the water. I tried to stop him because I wanted to look at it. I was to late!

We tried to visit with Violet and Theodore every year of two. They always took time to come and see us too. They had a house in the country. They had a big wheel barrow that the kids were trying to walk on, they had a horse that they all took turns riding, they had a pond and they went swimming. I remember we took a lot of movie films of these activities. Theodore was working in his extra time on his airplane. We took some pictures and every one tried to turn Dexter's face to see the camera. He was pretty young and after a while he got upset and told them to stop it.

Oh yes, I just remembered that was when we stopped and bought our first brand new car. It was a white Chevy. It had that wonderful new smell.

Carol had a big Cookie Birthday Party, I think she was 12. She invited all the girls in her class. She asked if she should invite the only black girl in her class. I said yes, that would hurt her feelings if she didn't. I made cookie dough, several colors of frosting and sprinkles for the girls to make and decorate their cookies. Each girl rolled and cut their cookies, they made 6 each. Cooked them and decorated them. Some had never cooked anything before. That party was a big success. They took their cookies home with them.

Lloyd's Grandma, Lilly Kathryn Wymer Adams, came to visit with us for a week. Every year when she came for a week, we bought her a complete set of clothes. She picked out a new dress, new shoes, and under clothes. One year she could not find shoes that fit her and that she liked. Just before it was time to take her home she wanted to shop for shoes again. We still couldn't find any that she liked. She said she had to buy some or she would not get any. So I just gave her the money and she was happy. I enjoyed it when she came, she always said she couldn't help much but she did know how to do dishes. We got along good together. I really liked her.

After about 3 years in Mexico, Missouri, the Manor Bakery notified us that all door-to-door sales were being discontinued. So Lloyd could move back to Kansas City and work in the bakery or look for other work. So Lloyd was without a job with 5 kids to feed.

One of Lloyd's men that worked with Manor Bakery applied to Ronnaco Coffee for a job as Sales Manager. The owner called Lloyd for a reference. Lloyd told him that the man was a good route man and with the proper training that he was sure he would be able to do the job. About 2 weeks passed, the owner called Lloyd again. He asked if Lloyd would come and hear what they could offer him.

Ronnoco is a Coffee Company and they sold all kinds of products to restaurants. We were on our way to meet the owner of the coffee company to get a job. They requested both Lloyd and me to come because we would both be going to business functions if we were hired. I bought a new coat before we went to St. Louis. I had needed one so this was a great chance to buy one.

On our way to St. Louis, Lloyd told me that when we got there, they would probably offer us some coffee. He told me to drink the coffee. Now I had never drank a cup of coffee in my life. Mother would never let us have it as kids and said it was an adult drink. When we were grown if we wanted to drink coffee, it was up to us. I had tasted it and did not like it. I guess it is like beer, you have to acquire a taste for it.

I explained to my husband that since I did not like coffee, it would be better to just explain it to the lady. For instance, if I offered someone a piece of chocolate cake that I had made and they tasted it and did not eat it, I would think it was not good. But if they explained that they were allergic to chocolate, I would not think anything of it. He said, "Drink the damn coffee!"

When we got to their home, it was a beautiful big house. We were invited inside. She and I sit on the couch, she went into the kitchen, and she came back in with a big beautiful coffee set. She offered me a cup of coffee. I never looked at Lloyd. Oh dear, I'm in trouble again..............

I said, "No, thank you, coffee smells so good but I have never acquired the taste. My mother would never let us children drink coffee because it was an adult drink." She asked if she could get me some juice or a coke. I said, "I really would just like a drink of water." She got a glass of cold water and then poured the men a cup of coffee. Lloyd never spoke of it again and neither did I. You know I still think I did right. We were together at many conventions and dinner meetings and she would have known after all those years, I did not drink coffee. We were hired any way. We moved to St. Louis and Lloyd was Sales Manager over four states. He was gone a lot more of the time.

We built a new three level house in Creve Coeur with a basement. I had my new stove built into the kitchen. We had three bedrooms and two baths upstairs, and two bedrooms with one bath in the recreation room in the lower level. In the basement, we had our washer, dryer, pool table, and furnace. We were on the far west side of town. We picked that area because Lloyd would be working a lot west of where we would be living.

They just started building the road. It was going to be called 270 because it joined with I-70. The highway is from Kansas City I-70 on past Illinois.

We could not move into our home because it rained the night before we got to Creve Coeur. The road was too muddy to move in our house. We called Uncle Clair and Aunt Lavern and told them our problem. They said, "Come on over; we have room for all of you." We stayed a couple of nights with them. Uncle Clair was Daddy's older brother. When the road dried, we moved into the house. The electricity was not even installed to the house. They stretched an electric wire from a neighbor's house and it was only a couple of days till we were hooked up.

One of the first things I saw and did not like was that there was no coat closet. I stopped one of the men that was working and asked if they could put in a coat closet by using the extra space in the entry? So they added the coat closet and a space facing the kitchen turned into a small pantry at my suggestion. I noticed they did that in every house they built later.

We had a lot of company when we first moved to St. Louis. I didn't realize it but Lloyd suggested that I go and visit Oliver. He said I was getting crabby and that wasn't me. Peggy was about three at that time. I flew to Olivers and had a nice visit with Oliver, Dorothy and their three kids.

They were living in San Antonio at that time. The picture on the wall is Olivers family.

Here is a picture of me at Oliver's wearing the dress Carol loved. I had lost 28 pounds in 1968 while I was president of Weight Watchers. Carol

thought I looked like Jane Russell and she asked me to pose for a profile picture. I have lost weight many times but finally gave up because I always got pregnant!

I liked living in Creve Coeur. My Uncle Clair and Aunt Lavern lived in St. Louis. It was like having parents again. They would come over about every other Sunday for dinner. They never stayed long. They didn't want to impose. One day Uncle Clair brought us a Mimosa tree. Lloyd and Uncle Clair planted it in the front yard, but it was good memories.

The next thing I knew was that I was expecting another sweet baby. I was not upset but I did want a girl. I had all my friends praying for me to have a girl. Three boys were enough. Polly needed a little sister. I was praying for a girl. In those days you didn't know until the baby was born.

Carol and Danny had dated all through High School and College. Danny was the youngest child in their family. He was really excited. They let me know every time they left the house where they were going. One day I called them to come home and stay with the other kids. Lloyd was home and took me to the hospital. I was waiting for him at the door. Lloyd finally got to take me to the hospital, for the first time.

Peggy Sue was born April 17, 1966 in St. Louis at the Saint Marys' hospital. She weighed 7 pounds. I never gained over 20 pounds with any of the children. Then I had to work and try to lose the extra pounds. Peggy was such a sweet and cute little girl. She was just like a pretty doll.

My Doctor was on his vacation, so we had a substitute Doctor that I had not met before. His nurse tried to give me a shot, but I said no. I didn't need a shot to relax me. I had already had two babies natural and did not need the shot.

The Doctor insisted and gave me the shot anyway. It was the Twilight shot to make me relax. It made my mind drunk; I could not think what I was supposed to do. The pain was worse. I could not think to relax. This was the

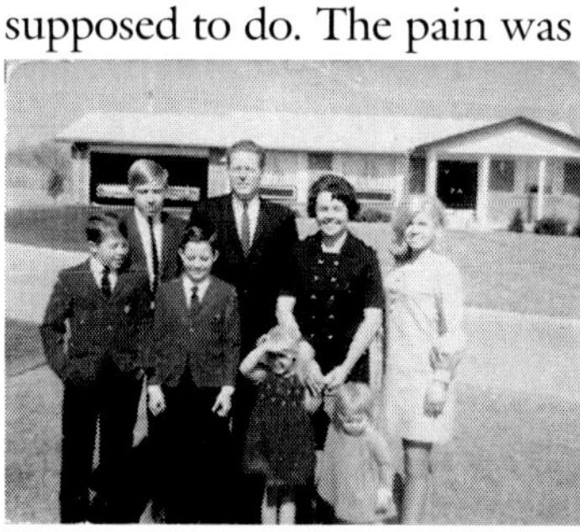

hardest and hurt more than any of the others, just because I could not think to relax. Think of whatever helps you to relax. For me it was to water ski. I liked the small spray of mist in your face ridding right behind the boat. I water ski when I go to the Dentist or anything that might hurt.

Polly needed a sister. She was getting a little spoiled with all the attention. Polly is about 3years and 4 months older than Peggy. and all the girls were blonds. Jerry and Dexter both had brown hair. Oliver asked me one time, "Do you know what causes having all those babies?" I answered, "Yes, it is that moving all the time." Peggy is one and half in this picture, with the other children.

Don and Pat Webb were good friends of ours. We both went to the same church. They had two children, Andrea and Scott. Scott was a good friend of Dexter's. We played Pinochle together almost every Friday night.

Pat and I went shopping together once in a while. I was always looking at wedding rings. Our 25th Wedding Anniversary was coming and I was hoping this year I'd get a wedding ring. I picked one out that was so pretty. It had three rows of diamonds with the middle ones just a little bigger. It was a one carat total diamonds.

As the sales lady was putting it away, she put it beside a bigger ring. It looked just like the first one but it was a two carrot total diamond ring. I didn't know it but Pat wrote down all the information and gave it to Lloyd and told him to buy it for me.

Surprise he did buy it for me! I had been without any wedding ring for three years. He gave it to me the night before our Anniversary. I have had it 43 years and I still love it! I don't know who was the most surprised, Oliver or me.

Oliver was really impressed that Lloyd bought it for me. Oliver always acted like I was just his little sister and Lloyd was the poor boy across the field. That night when Lloyd gave me my 25th Anniversary ring he changed. Oliver was so impressed when Lloyd gave me the beautiful two carat diamond ring with 17 diamonds in it. He really changed, Lloyd was successful, and I had finally grown up.

Oliver was impressed with our friends too. We had friends from Lloyds work, friends from our old Railroad days, friends from our neighborhood, and Family. I was proud of all of them. They talked and mingled all evening long. Everyone gave us beautiful silver gifts, and Lou Belcher made a beautiful 3 layer Wedding cake.

My kids were great too. Carol was the hostess and greeted everyone at the door; Jim, Jerry and Danny were attending the bar, Dexter, Polly and Peggy were the cleanup crew. They picked up the dirty dishes, and any trash around.

Several months later Lloyd's parents celebrated their 50th Anniversary. They held open house at the church. Many of their Friends came and celebrated with them.

Herb and Sarah had six children, Charles, Lloyd, Thelma, Anna, Marjorie, and John. Julia, Charles wife, did most of the work for their party. Several of Pop and Mom's friends and relatives came to congratulate them.

Lloyd made a strawberry bed in the back yard. He made it 3 tiers high, the biggest, one a little smaller and then another box a little smaller than the last one. It worked pretty well and was easy to pick strawberries. Later Polly or Peggy brought a small start of a tree from school. Lloyd planted it on the top of the strawberry bed.

I happened to be home when they came to grade our yard in St. Louis. I ran out and told him how to do it so the kids would have a level yard to play on, not a hill. Everyone else in the whole subdivision had a hill for their yard. Ours was terraced so we had a level area for our patio, then a sloop to a level yard for the kids to play. They liked to play croquet and tennis.

I was fixing up the house and decided that I wanted cornices over the living room windows. I asked Lloyd to help me make them one Saturday. He said OK, but never did get to it. After a couple of weeks, I decided I could do it myself. I went to the lumber yard, told the man the measurements of my windows and He told me how to do it. I bought the things I needed and went home and made them. After I got them all made, I called a girl friend to come and help me put them up. I needed someone to hold one end while I connected the other end. I was quite proud of my job. It looked good when I got through.

We were the fourth family in our subdivision. I made it a point to take some cookies and introduce myself to each new neighbor. We had a subdivision swimming pool, basketball court and plenty of room for the kids to play just across the street behind the houses. It was a great place to live. Most of my kids swam on the swim team. Later most of them were life guards. Our kids were growing up.

Twylia + Children - 2008

We had a new neighbor next door to us. They bought Craig and Marilyn Jensen's house next door. The new neighbors moved in after we had lived there several years. I went over and introduced myself and took them cookies that I had made. I invited them over any time, someone was always home. They had 2 children. About 2 months went by, and one day they came to our back yard to visit. They had finally realized we were not going to invade them with my 6 kids. We almost always had neighbors drop over to visit in our back yard. Lloyd always had beer for the men to drink. Most of the ladies just had ice tea or cokes.

Lloyd had worked in the Saint Louis area and was successful building sales and decided to start working more in the Kansas City area. He called on Tom Gault in Kansas City. Tom had two big business restaurants. Lloyd and Tom became good friends but he did not change coffee for Lloyd. He told him when the Coffee man that he had now quit he would change coffee company's.

We started going on some trips together. Tom, Bettie, Lloyd and I all got along great together. One day Tom called Lloyd and said come on and put your coffee in my restaurants. The other man was finally promoted to Texas and had moved.

We went on many trips together. We covered most of the states in the United States, all except North Dakota..

The first time we went to Hawaii was very interesting for me. I had never flown before on a big airplane, as I got on the plane I stopped and looked in at the cockpit.

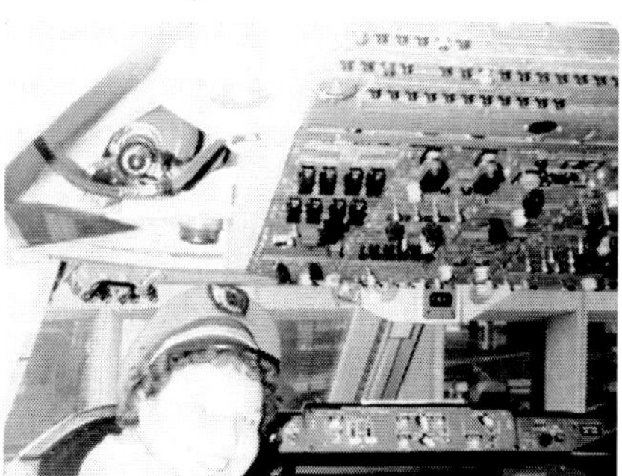

The Pilot was still there, he told me to have a seat and put his hat on my head. So I really got to see the dash board and the front of the plane pretty good. Bettie took my picture with the pilot's hat on my head, I was acting like I was the pilot.

Lloyd complained about it costing too much, and the trip was too long. I said I would pay for the trip out of my money. We landed and Lloyd looked at the pretty flowers and loved Hawaii.

Tom and Bettye Gault had a condominium on the 2nd floor looking straight at a cove in the ocean. We snorkeled in that cove every morning. Everything in the ocean is alive. We saw all kinds of fish, one of the fish looked like pencil. Later I asked a man if there was a fish that looked like a pencil. He said yes there was one that was long and very small around. Lloyd took some crackers and fed the fish. They all swam around him for more food. We all did a lot of sight seeing, swimming, and enjoyed it all.

Jan. 26, 2002 Tom Twylia + Bettye Gault

Dole Company always had the big Pineapple plantation. The pineapple were so sweet. I always took a carrier home with four pineapple back home. When we ate out they always put about 4 pineapple fingers on our plates. We loved Hawaii. We loved to swim in the ocean.

Pineapple Harvesting in Hawaii

One year we had Lloyd's whole Family come to our house for Thanksgiving. He bought a cooked pig with an apple in its mouth, and it had cherries for its eyes. Everybody enjoyed the pig. None of us had ever eaten a whole pig before. It was a small pig but plenty big for all of us. His Folks came from Fredonia, Kansas. Some of his brothers and sisters came. We all had a good visit and dinner. I think all the Adams was there but John's family andThelma's family. Thelma's family lived in Colorado. The family still talks about the time we had a pig.

Lloyd called me one afternoon; he had a wreck on I-70 coming home. He was not hurt but the car was a total loss. He was coming over a big hill that had ice on it. He slid down the hill and hit some other cars that had done the same thing. He had hit the window with his elbow and broke the window. But on the phone he kept saying don't worry, I am not hurt. He got another company car right away. He did hurt his elbow and arm. It was hurt but not broken.

Lou · Janet · Patty + Twylia

I had learned to Bowl in Mexico, so I signed up on a ladies league right away in St. Louis, I was lucky and got on a good team. Our team members were Lou Belcher, Janet Barret, and Patty Goldman. We won several tournaments. One day I yawned while I was a substitute on a different league.

Betty, one of the girls, asked if I was up late last night. I told her that we had played bridge and after we played, we just sit and talked pretty late. She asked me if I could get another person to play bridge if she got one too. I said yes. Then she asked if I could have it at my house. I said yes again. That was the beginning of four of us playing every Friday for ten years. It was Betty, Joan, Ramona and Me. After about a year, Ramona had to quit, she was pregnant, and Donna Bledsoe joined us.

The four of us became like sisters. We shared our joys and our sorrows. One morning Donna came in about to cry. We asked her what the matter was. Her daughter was just beginning to develop and one side was growing but the other side was not. We all laughed and said just give her a little more time.

Ramona had a baby that had both sex organs. They had to decide whether to have her become a boy or a girl. They chose a girl. I think the operation to fix her was easier. I had heard of this happening but didn't know anyone that it happened to before. I have often wondered if they made the right decision.

Peggy was little so I always had bridge at my house. The girls all took turns bringing lunch. We started playing about 9:30 AM and quit about 3:00 PM. In the summer lunch was a salad or sandwich. In the winter we had casserole dishes. We were trying to keep it simple. The hours were great to play while the kids were in school.

Joan was a very good player. She taught the rest of us a lot about Bridge. We played every Friday for about ten years. Betty's husband retired and they moved to Florida on the west side of Florida. A short time later Joan's husband retired and they moved to the east side of Florida. So our little group fell apart. I really missed them, we had grown so close. Later both Betty and Joan died of cancer. I think of them often. We were great friends. We had a lot of fun together.

One time when we had four kids, we went to Monterey, Mexico sight seeing. We hired a young man to be our guide. He was a very good guide. He showed us the usual things to see. It also included a grave yard. It was all decorated pretty with artificial flowers on most of the grave stones. I was surprised to see a bone pile in a cemetery. If the relation did not pay their grave rent, the bones were dug up and burned in the bone pile in the corner of the cemetery. Then the owners would rent the grave to someone else.

The Mexicans had just finished building a cable car from one mountain to another mountain. It was finished and the builder and some important men were to be the first passengers to try it out. They were about half way across and it broke. They were all killed. I had said it might be fun to go across on it. It was not open to the public yet. Thank God.

We were amazed that along some long roads you never saw a house, but you could see someone walking. There were very few cars. We couldn't figure out where they were going or where they came from to be on the road. There were no houses you could see or no town. Sometimes they would disappear but we never did see where they went or was going.

We bought several souvenirs in Mexico. Jim had to have a big sombrero. It was a good trip except for one thing. Lloyd had brought a gun from his folk's home and it was in the trunk. We had to check the gun in a cabinet at the customs area. Then we had to return the same way to get it back. It was our first good family trip on a vacation. We all enjoyed seeing Mexico.

Jim served in the Army during the Koran war. When he came home he brought a friend he had in the Army from California. The man's brother was Bill Imhoff, a St. Louis Cardinal Player. Jim asked if he could invite Bill Imhoff and Conrad Dabbler, another, Cardinal player, over for a Sunday dinner when they were not playing. I said of course, any time you want. He invited them over.

Sept 20, 1972

St Louis Cardinals

Dexter was 10 years old. He was so excited they were coming over. Actually we all were excited. I fixed 6 fried chickens, Jim said "Mom that won't be nearly enough." So I ended up fixing 14 Fried Chickens, a huge bowl of mashed potatoes, a big bowl of Gravy, Green beans, corn, salad, Two big Pans 10 X14 of home made light rolls, and 4 pies. Every bite was eaten. They really enjoyed home cooking. I sure would not like to cook for them all the time. I took Dexter's picture with the two football players. He wore it out showing it to all his school friends. I didn't have another picture of them with Dexter, so I couldn't put the picture in my book.

It was so good to have Jim home again. Jim went to College in Columbia University after he got home from the Army. He decided that he should use his GI benefit for his education. Mary went to Columbia and moved in with him. When he quit school they both returned to St. Louis.

While we were living in St. Louis, I decided to work on our Family Tree. I sent all the relatives a form letter asking about their own immediate family. I asked them to send me back the information. Some of them did send me the information but most of them did not. I put together what I could and made a small note book of the information.

Leonard + Ruann Clinesmith

We always went to the Clinesmith's family reunion every two years. It was called the Clinesmith Reunion but most of it was actually the Bentley's that married into the Clinesmith Family that kept it going.

That next year I took the family book that I had put together. Everyone was looking at the book. Some said, "You don't have us in your book!" I told them to send me the information. Several sit down and wrote what they could right then. As I got information, I would add it to the book. Now I have a great big book on our Past History. As time went by I started working on the Adams Family and the Dexter Family. Now that most of us have a computer I hope someone keeps the books current.

Time changes all things. We still go to the Clinesmith Reunion but now it has changed to really being the Clinesmith Reunion. The Bentley's have mostly died out or quit coming. The younger Clinesmith's have done most of the work to keep it going.

Oliver and Dorothy used to always stay with Calvin and Rena Clinesmith's. Lloyd and I would stay with Raymond and Mary's. Bless them for their hospitality. I still go to Raymond and Mary's for the reunions. Usually I drive and take a friend with me so I don't have to travel by myself. It is more fun that way and it gives us a good visit.

Lloyd was gone traveling most of the time. We only get together on most week ends. Lloyd asked the company to move us to Kansas City so he could increase the business in that area.

We moved to Blue Springs, Missouri. We wanted to stay in Missouri because we had Dexter still in College. When we moved to Blue Springs only three children went with us, Dexter, Polly and Peggy. Polly and Peggy were both in High School. Dexter was in college in Warrensburg, Missouri. He graduated with a degree in Business.

Lloyd and Tom had become good friends. Tom and Bettye owned a time share and traveled a lot. They started inviting us to go with them. When their regular Coffee man was transferred Tom called Lloyd and said he was ready to change to Ronnoco.

Carol married Danny Joe Carr on Janurary 24, 1970. Carol and Danny lived in Rolla, Missouri while Danny was going to College studying to be an Engineer. Carol worked until their little boy, Jeffrey was born on July 13, 1973. We could not wait to see and visit with them and play with that sweet baby. After I had children for so many years, I wondered how I would be with Grandchildren. I should have not worried; they all are such a blessing. Now when they cry, you can give them back to Mother or Daddy.

Jeffrey attended College at Texas A & M, in Commerce, Texas. He was active in his college and was President of his Fraternity, Delta Tau Delta. He was looked upon by his class mates as a good leader. Jeff had a Double Major in Marketing and Management. After he graduated he bought a house in

Frisco, Texas. He helps people get jobs, he works for HLP Solutions. Jeffrey has not married yet.

Kelly Ann Carr was born Dec. 7, 1974, in Garland, Texas. Kelly **attended the North Texas University.** She joined Chi Omega Sorority. When she graduated from College, she started working for Starmark Advertising Company. She was very active in school. She was a drill team leader in High School.

Kelly married Sean Arash Souri, on April 15, 2006 in Dallas, Texas. Sean and his family were from Tehran, Iran. They have two children, Noah Kamran Souri and Sophia Lili Souri.

We went to the horse races one time with Carol and Danny. Danny set it up for all of us with his friend. I think we had the best seats. After the races they had a great fireworks display.

As you can see Sophia is a little baby. This is our 4 generation picture. I guess it is time to take another picture since I am still alive and running. It was taken at the horse race.

4 Generations = Twylia, Carol, Kelly, Sophia

Carol became quite an artist. She decorated her children's bedrooms. The neighbor lady came over and asked her to paint and decorate her children's bedrooms. The ladies husband was a store manager from Kroger Grocery store. He hired Carol to paint and decorate the walls and windows of his store, then later all the Kroger stores. She painted all the windows for the special holidays. She had to hire helpers to do that much work. After a couple of years the Manager was told that even if all the customers liked her work, it was becoming too expensive.

One Christmas she drew designs for out door decorations. Danny cut the designs out in wood. Carol painted the wood in different Christmas designs of animal characters for a whole subdivision. They were all made in wood and probably still used at Christmas time. Carol and Danny are both very active in their social life.

One Christmas while we were still at the Lake of the Ozarks,

I went through all my picture albums and took a lot of the pictures out of my album. Then I got each child a small album of their own. I started with each child a baby. Then they could add pages when the child grew older. Each of the children was so pleased with their pictures. They spent most of the day looking at each other's albums. I requested that they add a picture every so often to keep the albums up to date. Now I am writing this book and I have already given the kids most of my good pictures.

Jim married Mary Busman and they bought a home in Manchester, Missouri. Jim had a great opportunity to go into business with his brother in law. Mary's brother was the business man and Jim was the sales person. Jim did very well in his business. He read and heard our records about selling. We loaned him the money to help them get started in the business. He paid back every penny with interest. We were very proud of him and his success. Jim told us one time that he could not fail. He had a salesman for a Dad, with Ronnoco Coffee Company, and a saleswoman for a Mother in Real Estate.

Jim and Mary had one little boy. His full name was James Charles Adams. He was born May 4, 1982 in St. Louis. Jim was so proud of his little boy. He took him every place he could. Mary quit coming to our home but Jim and Jimmy came to every big event and special holiday. Jimmy enjoyed the lake like our other kids did. They all loved to swim, Water Ski and just have a lot of fun.

Jim developed cancer. The cancer would respond to the treatments and all looked good. Then the cancer came back again. Jim went through this off and on, over and over. He had the treatments several times and the cancer kept coming back. When it came back the last time he told the Doctor to just let him die.

My whole family went to be with him at different times. Carol and Peggy spent the night in the hospital with him. Jim asked, "Carol why haven't I died yet?" She answered, "Jim we are here to be with you, weather you live or die we will be with you." The nurse said that just a drop of water could prolong his life. He was in the hospital about a week while we visited with him. We had just gone home and Jim died. I have learned your heart can break lots of times. Lloyd and I went to Jim's funeral in St. Louis. Mary didn't make us feel very welcome. The kids had to go on home to work. Marjorie sent me a nice flower arrangement to the funeral. I did get to keep that one flour arrangement.

As years passed our Jimmy became Jim, after our Jim died, our Grandson became Jim. Jim is grown now and he lives in an apartment in St. Louis. Jim got a job calling on Doctors and giving them samples of medicine. I think now he's back working in his Dad's company. His Mother Mary is still living in the house that my Jim and Mary bought in Manchester. My Jim taught Mary to play golf and she is still very active at their country club.

Jerry went to College in Columbia, Missouri. He went two years and quit. He moved back to St. Louis. After a while he started back to College in St. Louis. This time he graduated on the Dean's Honor Roll.

Jerry and Mary went to Hawaii to get married. They had their Reception on a boat on the Mississippi River when they got back home.. It was a big reception and we just about filled the boat. Jerry and Mary had one little girl, Melissa. Melissa Ryan was born Dec. 26, 1991 in St. Louis, Missouri.

Mary wanted to become a nurse. She and Jerry worked it out where she went to school in the day time and Jerry worked at night in Balabans Bar. They asked me if I thought that would work. I said, "I don't know, when do you get to see each other?"

To make a long story short, Jerry and Mary got a divorce. Neither one has remarried. The last I heard Mary is living with a Doctor. She did become a Nurse.

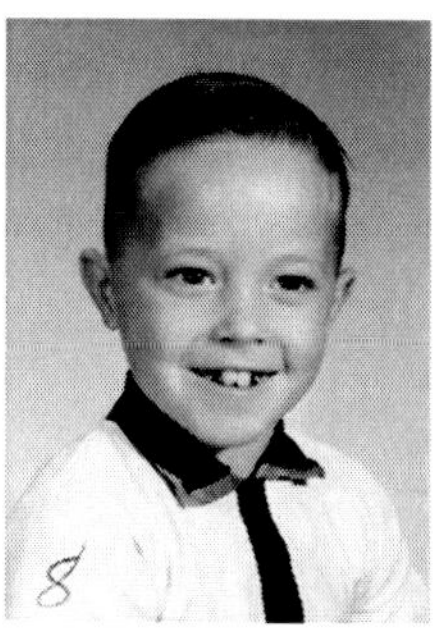

Jerry is still a bachelor; his life seems to be with his daughter, Melissa. When Melissa was in College, Jerry moved and bought a condominium in Hazel Wood, Missouri. It was a two story house with three bedrooms. He had a bath up stairs and down on the first floor. He let Melissa use the other house and rent rooms to her friends in college. It seems to be working out pretty good for both of them.

Jerry worked for a Truck Company in St. Louis. He had to drive to Kansas City and return to St. Louis each day. Then he got a different job with the same company, now he just drives in St. Louis and moved the truck's around. He moved the trucks getting them ready for the drivers to go on the road.

Dexter and Susan met in Warrensburg, Missouri in College. After they graduated from College, they got married. Susan taught school for a while and Dexter worked for an Insurance Company. He set Lloyd and me up with Midland Investment Company on an Annuity. We are still with them and so far doing well.

They had two Children. Aaron Andrew was born June 6, 1988. They wanted children and it seemed they couldn't have a child. So they adopted Aaron. Aaron was a really good looking kid as he grew up. He seemed very smart.

They learned that if they wanted to have their own blood child that Dexter could deposit his seed in the bank and Susan would go in and have it deposited in her. They did conceive a child and had a sweet baby girl.

Amber Ann was born March 17, 1991. They lived in St. Charles, Missouri. They had a lovely tri-level house on a big corner lot. It had horse heads decorating the fence around their house.

Susan decided that Aaron needed to go to a special school for his talents. She chose Troy, Missouri. They bought a nice mobile home and moved it on a big lot. Dexter had a lot of work to do to get the yard and house like they wanted it to be. Susan started selling Real Estate. Dexter worked as an investor.

The next thing I heard was they were getting a divorce. Susan did not love Dexter any more. Dexter took all of this real hard. He never did get over it.

I guess she had met this friend in Real Estate school. Aaron was not going to a school for special education. It was just another school. Maybe it was closer to her folks. It sure was a lot of extra work for Dexter.

Susan took a boyfriend to Amber's graduation from High School with her. Dexter asked Aaron why he didn't tell him that she was that interested in someone else? Aaron said he didn't want to hurt him. Neither Dexter nor Susan has married again.

Dexter moved to Jefferson City in Missouri. Several years later Dexter got Sugar Diabetes and was not as careful about what he ate as he should have been. He was working in a Gym and stubbed his toe. It would not heal so they had to amputate his small toe. Several years later one of his Neighbors invited him to a party for the whole apartment building. He went and had a great time. Later that night he had a reaction from something that he had eaten and he died that night.

Dexter was born April 10, 1957 in Independence, Kansas. He died 12/10/2010 in Jefferson City, at age 53.

We tried to visit with Oliver, Dorothy and their children at least once a year. We would go when we had a vacation or at least 3 days to visit. It was kind of hard to keep in touch when the kids were growing up. They would be in school or Lloyd would have to work. Each year we would try to go see them or they would try to come and see us. They lived in Dallas, Texas most of their married life.

One year we went to Dallas to see Oliver and family at Christmas time. Cindy was small then and she wanted a roll of toilet tissue for Christmas. It was a fun joke for all of us. She got it, just what she wanted. I don't remember what anyone else got but we had a great time.

Linda was the oldest of the kids. She was born first 1948 in Lawrence, Kansas. Carol was born in 1948 in Van Buren, Arkansas. Russell was born next in 1949 in Topeka, Kansas. Jimmy was born in 1951 in Claremore, Oklahoma; Jerry in 1955 in Nowata, Oklahoma, Cindy was born in 1956 in Manhattan, Kansas. Dexter was born April 10, 1957 in Independence, Kansas. The kids all were close enough that they enjoyed being together. It seemed every other child was Oliver's or ours.

Russell and Sandy Dexter live in International Falls, Minnesota. They invited us up to visit with them but we never got to go. Linda is living in South Carolina, and Cindy Jo lives here in Dallas.

While we lived in Blue Springs the Kansas City Chiefs won the American league. And the St. Louis Cardinals won the National League. They had a play off for the grand Champaign's. I called Jim and said I thought we should make a bet on the game. Jim said "Make it easy on you, St. Louis will win." I agreed with him, they probably would win. He came up with this idea; if I win he would take me out to a nice restaurant for steak. If he won, I would make a big freezer of home made ice cream with chocolate fudge to pour over it.

The final night of the games was over about eleven PM. I called him and he answered, "Hello MOM!!!" The Kansas City Royals WON. He paid off his bet about a month later when he could get up to see us. We had a lot of fun with the bet. He got hit pretty hard. He bought steaks for Lloyd, me, Peggy, his son, Jimmy and himself.

Lloyd was home more after we moved to Blue Springs. I joined A bowling league again. I was a fair bowler. I had an average of 157. I had won a Dutch 200 game. The patch was in the shape of a wooden Dutch shoe. I also won a Strike and then a spare game clear across the board. I got a patch for that too. I forgot what that one was called. We won several patches for winning tournaments. I still have my shirt with all my patches.

I hadn't lived in Blue Springs long when I called Welcome Wagon and asked if they could come and see me as I was new in town. She said they did not have a hostess in Blue Springs now. About 2 weeks later she called back and asked if she could take me out to lunch. Of Course I said yes. We met and she tried to talk me into being the new welcome wagon hostess. I told her I would think about it. She asked me to come to the training and find out about it and then decide. I asked her if I could have helpers. I didn't want to cover the whole town by myself. She said yes but they needed the training too.

The next time I bowled I talked it over with my team members and asked if they would like to be a Welcome Wagon hostess. They surprised me and all of them agreed to go and try it too, so we all went to the training. One day at the training, I found that you could get a car to drive if you represented a car dealer. I told my boss that I was going to get a car. She said no, that is the hardest sell of all the businesses.

When Lloyd came home, I talked it over with him. I thought if I can do this job I could get a car. If I couldn't maybe I shouldn't be a Welcome Wagon Hostess. Lloyd said, "Do what you want to, then you would know." The next morning, I called and made an appointment with a car owner, Mr. Balderson, at the Ford Dealership.

I went on my appointment and I gave him the whole sales pitch. He said my boss had tried before to get his business. I asked if she got him and he said no. I said, "Then she was not a very good salesman if she didn't get your business." He said, "I thought she was a good sells person." I told him, "I am going to get a car dealer, if not you, then one of the others." He asked, "What kind of car do you want?" I said, "Whatever you want me to sell" He asked, "Is a pinto station wagon good enough." I said, "Yes, that would be great. REALLY?" I was so excited. He said the Pinto Station Wagon would be ready for me to drive in two days. The reason for waiting two days is they put a big notice and our picture in the paper. Needless to say, my boss at Welcome Wagon was very surprised when I told her.

Welcome Wagon Gets New Hostess

I drove a new Pinto Wagon each year for two years and I know I sold several cars. Welcome Wagon is an advertising company. I had to get my own sponsors to represent on my calls. My job was to get the people in their store and it was up to them to keep them as customers. The other girls would not even try to get the new customers, but they were happy when I got new ones.

When I called on the new people in town, they always asked, "Who is a good Doctor" and 'Who was a good Dentist?' I was not allowed to tell them because at the time they could not advertise. Before I left, I had usually told them where I bowled and I went to the husband of a friend for my Dentist. After several years the Dentist sent me a "Thank You" note saying I had sent him most of his customers. Later on a Sunday while he was playing Tennis, I got a pork chop bone caught between my teeth. He quit playing and met me at his office and got the bone out. Then he went back to play tennis.

Another time the Blue Springs Bowling Alley gave me a big bowling pin trophy for recommending the new comers to go bowling at their alley. I was surprised at that because I was just trying to help the new people to get acquainted in their new town.

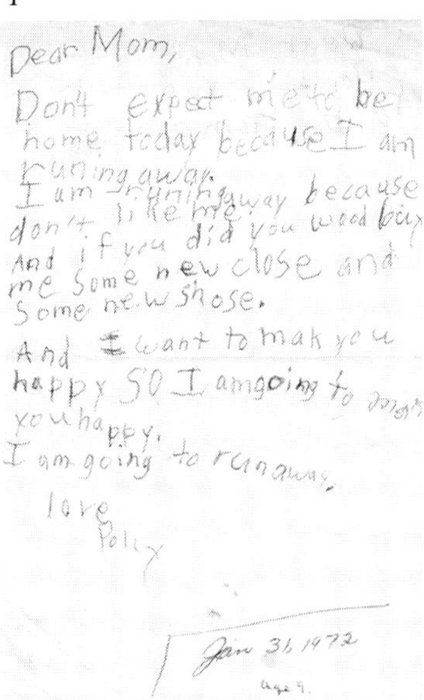
Dear Mom,
Don't expect me to be home today because I am runing away.
I am runing away because don't like me. if you did you wood buy
And if you
me some new close and some new shose.
And I want to mak you happy SO I am going to mak you happy.
I am going to run away.
love
Polly
Jan 31, 1972
age 9.

Polly got married while we lived in Blue Springs. She wanted her Granddad Adams to perform the wedding. Polly and Dan Estrada were married in Fredonia, Kansas. They moved to Nebraska. Later they got a divorce, they had no children.

Polly married David Butzin and they had a little boy, Erik Lloyd, born Jan. 7, 1987 in Nebraska. They got a divorce.

Polly married Richard Leffler at our July Family reunion on July 3, 1994. Rich was born March 20, 1959 in Nebraska. They had three more children, Lacey Marie, Jan. 1994, Elijah James on Sept. 11, 1995, and Samatha Jean on April 25, 1997. Every one loves Richard, she finally found a keeper. Polly and Rich are good parents. Erik is the big brother to all the children. They have a wonderful family.

Polly's family - 7-4-2008

Since I was working with owners of companies I began to realize I needed to join the Chamber of Commerce to meet the business people. Shortly after I joined the Chamber they had a big New Member contest. The prize was four days in Los Vegas for two. I decided Lloyd and I should win and go on the trip. I was quite a ways ahead when I had to be gone for several days. When I got back home another girl had passed me. I only had two more days and the contest was over. I spent the next two days calling on businesses and won. Lloyd and I had a good time. We stayed in the Grand Hotel and it was deluxe. About a year after we stayed at the Grand Hotel, It caught fire and part of it burned. They remodeled and were open again.

While I was working for Welcome Wagon, I also got a Real Estate Company. Don Willsey, of Blue Springs Realty, asked what I could do for him. I told him lots of people rented for a while when they moved to town then bought a house. I would recommend that they would go to Willsey Real Estate to buy their house. So he joined.

After about a year as a customer, Don began to try to talk me into selling property for Willsey Real Estate. It was the best Real Estate Company in Blue Springs. I told him, I would like to do it but that Lloyd did not want me to work. I said I knew it but Lloyd thought I was just visiting with the new people in town. He asked me to have Lloyd come and visit with him. So we both went to see the broker.

Don asked Lloyd, "If you were to die could Twylia make a living selling for Welcome Wagon?" Lloyd laughed and said, "no". Don said, "With Real Estate she could."

Later at home Lloyd asked if I really wanted to sell Real Estate. I said yes. So he said then go ahead and give it a try. I said no. He would get upset with me if he ever came home and I wasn't there or if dinner was not ready. I could not work if I had to worry about that happening and he would be mad at me. He thought a minute and said "I promise not to get mad or upset." So I quit Welcome Wagon, gave back my Pinto Station Wagon and started to work in Real Estate. That was the smartest bargain Lloyd and I ever made. He surprised me and he never said a word if I got home late.

I was invited to join the Ladies Pilot club. It was a club of ladies doing service projects for Blue Springs. While I was in the club I helped my broker Don to start a Junior College in town. We went to several other clubs and organizations giving talks and showing diagrams of the possible college that we hoped to build. Later it passed and they did build a College.

Another project that I was interested in was to start a Life Line with the local Hospital. We also got that started. I asked that at least one unit go to a person free that needed it but could not afford one. The hospital agreed. I wonder if they are still honoring it.

I loved Real Estate. I would wake up in the morning excited to go to work. The first year I won the most sales for a new one year Realtor in the Greater Kansas City Area.

Due to my success in helping with the College and Lifeline with the Hospital, I was nominated as Citizen of the Year by the Pilot Club. It was a great honor. I did not win. The Superintendent of Blue Springs Schools won. At least I was in good company. Polly wrote me a wonderful letter telling me that even if I did not win, I was first in her life and she loved me. I kept that note it was so wonderful of her; I put it in my Picture Album.

The first year I was in Real Estate we had a convention in Los Vegas. I had been to Los Vegas before when Lloyd and I went together. It was fun but this time it was all about Real Estate. Zig Ziegler was the main speaker and he was real good and interesting. He is a great Motivational speaker. This was the second time that I had met and talked with him. Once he was on a tour with four other speakers. Art Linkletter, Zig Zigler, Rev. Schuler of the Chrystal Cathedral, and one more but I can't remember his name.

The 2nd year I was in Real Estate we had a Convention in New Orleans. Several of our Company went to the convention. One young couple that went asked me what they should take. I told them what I was taking, and I warned them to put most of their money in a safe place. There are always pick pockets at big conventions and places where there are a lot of people.

We flew to New Orleans and caught a cab to go to our Hotel. The young man whispered to me and asked if he could borrow the money to pay the cab. Of course I gave it to him. At the hotel he knocked on my door and gave me the money he borrowed. He said all his money was pinned to his shorts and he forgot to save some out to use. I advised him to keep enough in his pocket to buy whatever they needed.

Zig Zigler was the main speaker this year. I had met him before when the convention was in Los Vegas. He is a good motivational speaker. New Orleans has a huge convention center. They have all kinds of events held in the center.

They put on a complete Mondi Gras for us in the big convention center. The big parade, throwing beads, comics and everything just like their regular Mondi Gras.

The town tour with the others from our group was quite interesting. I saw things that I didn't even know what they were until I asked and then I was very embarrassed. The music was great. The entertainers were fun to hear and watch. Every little room had things going on. Don just kept swallowing the Clams and oysters. I couldn't stand to watch him! Over all it was a real good trip.

Ever since my parents left us kids at Grandma's I missed the love of my parents. Lloyd was a wonderful man, but he was not the passionate type. He was a good provider for the family. I explained to him many times that I missed him just saying he loved me. It just would have been good if he told me. He always said

"You know I do." I did know it, but I would have loved to hear him say it to me.

One day I was sitting in the office on duty. This young couple came in. They had sold a business for $20,000. They wanted to buy a house for the $20,000. I told them there was nothing in Blue Springs that cheap. They asked me to keep looking and let them know if I found something. They stopped in at the office several times but nothing had come up yet.

A couple of months later on tour day we looked at a house that the bank had repossessed. It was in very bad shape. It was listed for $45,000. New it would have been sold for $60,000. It was in a nice neighborhood. I called the couple and asked them to come in and let me show the house to them. They loved it even though it was torn up and in bad shape. He said he could repair the damage and fix it up. So we worked up a sheet to see what they could offer for the house. The most they could offer with the $20,000 down and a loan of $20,000. We wrote up an offer. When I presented it to the bank the bank president laughed. He said no. I explained that no one would buy it for what they had it listed for, and I asked him if he had seen it. He said, "No, he had not seen it, but the real estate man in the bank had." I told him to go see it, because if he turned these kids down he might have it for a long time. I would come back tomorrow for his answer.

He did go see it and accepted our offer. The young kids were so excited. I called on them about a month later and took them a gift. The house looked good. She was expecting another child. They had a little boy.

After another month I stopped in to see them again. She said the neighbors would not talk to them and would not let their children play with their little boy. I asked them if I could talk to them like a Mother, because I cared for them and wanted them to be happy. They said go ahead. I asked them if their neighbors said bad words and talked dirty like they did. They said no, that must be it. The neighbors didn't want their children to pick up the bad words.

About another month went by and I stopped in again. They were happy. I took their new baby girl a gift. I asked how the neighbors were now. They said just fine and real nice. I felt good that I helped raise their standard of living.

Lloyd and Tom remained good friends. One time Tom told us someone in his Restaurant was stealing his food from the restaurant. He set a trap to catch the Thief. He climbed up on the roof and laid in wait for the person. After everything was closed for the night, everyone had left but one man. The man carried out a lot of stuff to his car. Tom climbed down and caught him. He made the man bring all the food back into the restaurant and then he fired him.

One time we were going out with Tom and Bettye to a party. We were waiting for them to close up the restaurant. An older couple came in the Barn Restaurant with a plastic bag. They went through the line and filled their plate with just chicken. They came back to the table and put the chicken in her purse. Then they went back through the line again and filled their plates again. I told Bettye what we had seen and she said they do it all the time.

Tom had booked a convention to cater. It was a big deal and he couldn't take his employee's from the regular restaurants. He asked several of their friends to help out. Lloyd just stood and dished up dishes to pass around the table. I was a waitress. I had 2 tables of eight. Tom served steaks. I took my orders but forgot who ordered what. So I just passed them out. One man said, I ordered rare, another said he wanted medium, I told all of them to just pass them around until they got what they wanted. There were little plastic sticks in each one saying how it was cooked. They all passed until everyone was happy. I explained that I had never been a waitress before and they said they didn't mind. We went home and my feet were killing me. That was my first and last time as a waitress.

Our first trip with Tom and Bettye was to Fairfield, Arkansas. Their Time share was right beside the golf course. We spent a week seeing Fairfield and a lot of the surrounding area. Tom, Bettye, Lloyd and I all got along together and we had a good trip.

Several months later the Gaults invited us to go to Hawaii with them. This was in 1979. This was our another trip with Gaults. Lloyd said no, it is too far and cost too much. I said yes, I will pay for it all. He complained how long the flight would be for a month. Then it was time to go. We got on the plane. My sweet husband was still complaining.

We landed in Hawaii. Lloyd love d the beautiful flowers, he loved the view, and he loved everything he saw. You would have thought he had planned the whole trip. We stayed in the Hilton Hawaiian Village on the beach.

One of the first things we did was to go see the Arizona Memorial. When the Japanese attacked Pearl Harbor starting World War II, they sunk the battleship Arizona. The men were never evacuated from the ship. Lloyd fought the Japanese in Japan and in the Philippines. When Lloyd saw the Japanese looking at the Memorial he got real upset.

One **day we went to the** Polynesian Cultural Center. It was a good trip. They had canoes that went down a lagoon with each canoe carrying a King and a Queen from different tribes. They taught us to Hula, the coconut dance, and some other dance with sticks.

We ended up going with the Gaults on two trips to Hawaii. The second time we went to Hawaii, Lloyd didn't complain at all. There was a big round area of sea right in front of our condominium. We snorkeled every morning. It was great. Lloyd fed some crackers to the fish and they swarmed all around him. One morning Lloyd saw a baby octopus sunning on a rock way down on the bottom of the water. There were all kinds of fish. Everyday there were different things to see and do. I saw some fish that looked just like pencils swimming. At first I thought they were Sea Horses but they weren't. Later I asked a man if there were fish that looked like pencils, he said yes.

We went to the beach to swim. We were just standing there talking, I put my mask on and ducked under the water, there were long fish swimming all around us and we could not see them standing up. They were blue and matched the water.

Later that same afternoon, we were swimming and Tom did not swim so we all wore our life belts with him. He was just laying there floating on his back as we were talking. I noticed that Tom was drifting out to sea. I quickly told Lloyd to swim out and drag him back and don't tell him or he might panic. Lloyd saved him!

One Vacation we went with the Gaults to Virginia. On the way we stopped at Thomas Jefferson's home Monticello. It was truly amazing. Jefferson was way before his time. His house had things that were not even heard of then. He had a big clock in the front of his house. The slaves could see it from the grounds where they were working. It was outside and inside of the house. The long cables to wind the clock went down to the bottom floor through little holes in the corner of the room. The slaves pulled the cables to wind the clock from the down stairs. They had a Lazy Susan. It was a small elevator from the kitchen to the dining room. They could send the food up on the Lazy Susan, then serve it to the Family.

I always wondered why the beds were so short. I was told the people were short. No, they were not short. In those days they slept sitting up in bed. The pillows were stacked behind them. They were afraid if they lay down they would quit breathing.

Monticello had very narrow stairs going upstairs to the third floor. You better stay slim or you will not be able to go up on the stairs. All the cooking and help lived on the lower level. Also the stock was on that level too. From the front of the house it looked like a two story house. From the back of the house it was a three story house. The lawn was in perfect condition. To me it was a very interesting house. I didn't even realize that Thomas Jefferson was an inventor.

We saw about all of Washington DC., the Smithsonian, the Korea Memorial and the changing of the Guards at the National Cemetery and a lot of other stuff. Thanks to the Gaults' we did quite a few trips after Lloyd and Tom retired. While we were in Virginia we went to the Trappe Family resort. Marie was still living then and her youngest daughter lived with her on the Resort property. The Sound of Music Family was a true story and one of my favorites.

When we got to our condominium it had one big spacious bedroom and the other one had bunk beds. As we were the guests, we stayed in the bunk beds. I slept on top. I got up twice to go to the bathroom. The second time I just got in bed with Lloyd and told him to scoot over a little. That was better anyway.

We always have enjoyed all our trips with Tom and Bettye Gault. On one of our trips we went to Mount Rushmore. We went on to see the Indian. It will be a long way before that will be finished.

We were all set to go to Italy one year. I started having thoughts of my Uncle Clair, Daddy's brother. I just felt that he was either sick or going to die. I finally had the feeling so strong that I told the Gaults that we could not go to Italy. Betty said that's all right, we will go to California with you. We all went in their car. We visited friends and relation the whole way. It was so good to see and visit Uncle Clair and Aunt Lavern. Uncle Clair did look like he had been sick, but he was going strong. He wanted to show his garden to us. Anyone that wanted to could have a small space to grow their gardens. They were in an apartment building. Aunt Lavern looked good, she always looked the same. We didn't stay very long because I could see that Uncle Clair was getting tired. I told them I loved them and sure missed them after they moved from St. Louis.

We stopped in and visited with Eden for a while. Her husband, Evan had died. She invited her brother, Atlee and Bobby over for dinner and to visit for a while. The Gault's were at her cousin visiting until time for them to come and pick us up. Within just a year, Uncle Clair, and Atlee both had died. About another year later Aunt Lavern died. I had sent her a Birthday card and Eden answered it saying she had died about three months ago.

We saw Carlsbad Caverns, it was interesting and a very big Cavern. In the front of the Cavern the bats would come out in swarms. The caves were big, they had the Stalactite's, a deposit that drips down from the ceiling. They had the Stalagmite's, a deposit that projects up from the floor of the cavern. I learn a lot from our travels.

The Painted Desert,was so pretty with all colors of pretty sand.

The Petrified Forest, this was very interesting to me. The petrified wood had pretty streaks of all colors running all through the wood that had turned into rock. I bought a small piece of the rock to take home with me..

The Grand Canyon, I heard that they have built an extension from the viewing platform out over part of the Grand Canyon. It was good to see the Canyon but I could not be paid to go out on the platform.

Palm Springs, Lloyd and I played a game of golf there. Tom and Bettye just rode around and watched us play.

Knott's Farm was kind of like Silver Dollar City in Branson. I bought some of their Jelly. Of course it was good.

Disneyland is always fun. The main one was in California. The one in Florida was fun too though. They both had the Disney characters walking around greeting people. They had the different rides and many things to see. There ws lots of walking to see everything.

The Queen Mary, was a stationary ship that you could walk through and see the ship.

Howard Hugh's Spruce Goose, was covered and we could not see much there.

Robert Schuler's Crystal Cathedral was so pretty. The bells rang while we were just getting there. They always sound so pretty. We just heard about a year ago that the Crystal Cathedral had closed down because of financial reasons.

The Movie Star's homes were interesting. We went on the tour and the main ones that I remember was Lucille Ball's, and James Stewart's homes. They were both nice, and big but not a big show off type of place like some. We went to see where the movie stars put their hands and feet in the side walk on Sunset Strip, Beverly Hills.

Starting home we stopped at the Hearst Castle. It was a big castle with many big rooms for entertaining. The bedrooms were small. There was a big swimming pool, surrounding the pool was a lot of Greek statues that needed some clothes. Both the Men and the Women were nude. There were several small apartments for guests, separate from the Castle.

We walked on the Pebble Beach Golf Course, We saw the Sequoia Trees in Kings Canyon, Scottie' Castle, This man lived on the desert, He just kept adding to his house until he called it his Castle. We stopped in Las Vegas, we tried a little gambling, and went to a show.

We went to Zion National Park; we stood at the Four Corners in Utah, Colorado, Arizona, and New Mexico. We went on and visited the many forms of rock in the Monument Valley.

We had not lived at the Lake very long when we went on this trip. Several times Lloyd said he wished he was home; he needed to work on his yard. We were homeward bound with several stops to see yet, when we got to Fresno, California. Lloyd said he wished he was home again. Tom was driving and he just went to the airport and told Lloyd to go & fly home. The rest of us were having a great time. Lloyd beat us home by two days. He had a little trouble getting flights to go home.

We went through the Sequoia Trees in Kings Canyon after he left us. The first night we had trouble finding a motel. The first cabin they gave us was occupied; we walked in on them in bed. They were asleep until we opened the door and started in. We finally got one room with two beds. This was a great Vacation, one of the very best. We stopped in Los Vegas for one night and I gambled and lost a couple of dollars. Tom and Betty just looked around.

Another year the Gaults and we went to Colorado in the summer time. It was fun to see the ski runs and the lifts. The views were so pretty. We had a condominium there, The Breckenridge. Tom and Bettye had several time shares and we were so glad to go with them. I realized that my Birthday was just about here. I told Betty that Lloyd was not going to forget it this year. I told everyone that my birthday was in 8 days, then 7 days, 6 days, 5 days, 4 days, 3 days, 2 days, then the morning of my birthday, Bettie gave me a little rock with a small train on it. It was a memo of a train ride that we went on. Lloyd said, "Is today your Birthday? I forgot." I gave up!

Several years later we went to Hawaii again and we stayed in Kawai at a motel. We were deciding where to eat and decided that we would eat there at the motel. We went in to eat and the table near us was decorated up and we thought it was a wedding party. We found out that it was a Hollywood group filming "Fantasy Island." That was exciting. We watched them film the show where Ricardo Montebaum got married and she died in the same show.

They worked late at night so people would not bother them. They had both the little and big cars there. It took the workers several hours getting big gunny sacks placed so there were not any shadows showing on the water. They went through the whole show the first time. They announced that we could take pictures; however, when they started the second time, DO NOT TAKE any pictures. It would ruin the show.

Ricardo went over to the area where you could buy a beer or drink while they were waiting for the show to start again. Bettie and I went over and talked to him. We asked him where the little man was and if he would be there too. He said no, he wasn't going to be in that show. So we didn't get to see him. Ricardo had a limp when he walked, it never showed in the movies. If you ever noticed in the movies, he never took over two or three steps. He was real nice and very charming.

One afternoon we stopped at the restaurant for lunch. I looked at the lagoon right beside me. There were lots of little circles floating in the water. I threw some bread pieces in the water. It was fish swimming with their mouths open to catch food. Several years later a Hurricane came and wiped that motel off the map.

I was still working in Real Estate with Willsey Realty. Grandma called me one day while she was still living with Richard March my cousin. She called me to come and get her. Richard and his wife both worked and when they left she said they locked her in the house and she was afraid.

We went and picked her up and she stayed with us over a year. She would not go to the bath room soon enough. She would drip all the way to the bathroom. The house began to smell. I called Oliver in Dallas, then Aunt Jean in Wichita, Kansas. Neither of them would let her come to their house. I checked out the nursing homes near us. Oak Grove Missouri had a nice nursing home and it was run with the Country ladies working with the patients. I took her there. She seemed to like it and met the other ladies. She would be smiling and laughing with the other Ladies until she saw me then she would stop talking and pout. I went to see her twice a week and sometimes three times a week. I always took her fruit, cookies, something to be put in her drawer for later. She always griped about something to me.

One day when I arrived she asked me if she had any money left. I said yes a little. Did she need something? She said no. She wanted Kenneth Allen to have all her money. I asked her why. She said because he loves me! I told her OK. When she died, I gave her daughter Elva Jean ¼, Her daughter Glenna ¼, to her daughter, then I split Oliver and me ¼, the agreement with Uncle Carl, Grandmas son, was that when Grandpa died, if we would sell him the property reasonably, he would take care of Grandma the rest of her life, and would bury her. He never did buy her anything and then he died before she did. Aunt Oka, Carl's wife, did bury her when she died. Since I had taken complete care of her for over a year and paid for everything. I kept ¼ of the money to change my carpet. She didn't have that much to worry about and it didn't cover the new carpet.

Lloyd decided to have the company move him to the Lake of the Ozarks so we would be set to live there in retirement. I did not want to move. I loved Blue Springs and the Real Estate Business and did not want to quit. I knew all the business people and had a lot of good friends. I put him off for two years and he still wanted to move. So like a good wife, I finally agreed to move. Lloyd was still working but working to build business in the Springfield area. Just as we were moving the young couple called and had decided to move to the country. I referred them to one of the other girls in our office. I was proud of working with them even if it was the cheapest house I ever sold.

Lloyd was beginning to have trouble remembering things even before he retired. I read in the paper one day that Doctor Dexter at the Columbia Hospital in Columbia, Missouri was doing a study on Alzheimer's. I called and made an appointment for us to go see him. They talked with Lloyd and decided that he was a candidate for the study. I believe he was taking the real medicine because he got worse mentally very slowly. Some with people with that problem went much faster. Lloyd began to show me he cared; he knew he needed me to help take care of him. Our last few years were some of the best for me. He finally showed that he did love me.

We moved to Laurie, Missouri at the Lake of the Ozarks at the 10 mile marker. We found the perfect house like Lloyd wanted and got an acre of land on the water with a good 100 foot beach. I could walk fifteen steps in the water and it was at my nose whether the water level was high or low. That was because it was a man made lake in a mountainous area. The dam was built in two years by the PTA men in 1930. They built the dam using horses and wagons. They had the men clear the land up quite high; they thought this is crazy to clear the land so high. However when they filled it with water it was just right.

I told Lloyd the property had been on the market for at least two years and he couldn't sell it. So if he would let me handle it, I could get him to reduce the price. He said OK, he would keep quiet and let me handle it. We got out of the car, the man came out, and Lloyd went up to him and said, "This is just what I have been looking for!" Guess how much he came down on his price! I did manage to get him to reduce the price for what it would have cost him to pay a commission to a Realtor, and I handled the paper work.

The house had 4 bedrooms, 2 ½ baths, large living room and dining room with a fireplace and two large picture windows, looking at the lake. We had an office, a pool table room where we played cards too. When little kids came to visit we fixed them a bed under the pool table. We had several sleeping bed rolls. It had a fairly small kitchen but we could eat there, and a big utility room. There was a washer, a dryer, a refrigerator, freezer, trash compacter, furnace, hot water tank, a pass through window to our bedroom, lots of cabinets, & 2½ baths. We had two cabins. One large one with a king size water bed and a full size bed with kitchen and bath. The small one had a king size bed, a set of bunk beds, and bath with shower.

This is the lake view of our house at the Ozarks. It was shaped in a "L." We had the hot tub in the curve of the "L." We had a fireplace between the two big picture windows. I loved to sit on the breezeway and watch the boats go by.

We had a work shop with a water well. We had a trolley on a small railroad track; the trolley had three stops. From the main house, the first stop was at the well house. Next stop was at the cabins and then the dock. We had two boats; a fishing boat and a sixteen foot Cosby boat for everyone to water ski. Later we bought a pontoon boat. It was a lot more relaxing.

The house was perfect for our family. We had a bed for everyone. The kids loved to come and visit and play.

This is our dock. We had two boat docks to park the boats and a big sun deck. Lloyd made his fishing place at the end of the sun deck. There was a place to clean the fish in the sink. The beach was a perfect place to swim and play. I could walk out into the water and it took 15 steps to have the water touch my nose. The beach was small rocks and shells.

One summer when the kids were all home for the 4th of July, Jeff and Kelly stayed over for a week and visited with us. They each had a friend that was here too. We really enjoyed them and we all played, swam and had a great time. That was the only time that any of our Grandchildren stayed over and visited with us by themselves. I would have loved to have them but it just didn't seem to work out. It seems that now in the summer time there is so much for the kids to do.

The first winter we retired we went to Florida. We stopped in at Dewey & Sharon Valentine's, my cousin's home. They lived in Tavares, Florida. They lived in a Mobile home park. There was a canal right by their home. Dewey had a boat and took us for a ride down the canal. He showed us high trees with big ocean birds nesting in the top of the trees. Some alligators' were sitting around, it was really interesting. He said the first Tarzan movie was made there. It would have been kind of scary if it had gotten dark. When we got back there was an Alligator on a little low shelf right in front of their house, it was sleeping. The shelf was low enough that the alligator could not get up in the yard. I think!

We visited with Betty Henley and her husband on the west side on Florida, and Joan & Gene Tomlinson on the east side. They were both my old bridge friends from St. Louis. Betty and Joan have both died of cancer so I am glad we got to go see them when we did. We enjoyed seeing our Friends that had moved there but over all we did not like it there. The people seemed unfriendly to us. Also the weather was not good, it rained a lot.

The second winter we went to McAllen, Texas. I told Lloyd that Aunt Trilla and Uncle Herbert Valentine always invited us but we couldn't go then. So this was the time to go and see McAllen.

We found a mobile park called Adobe Wells Country Club, where most of the homes were permanent. There was a 18 hole par three golf course. Lloyd was in heaven. He could walk over and play golf any time he wanted to go play. We both played Golf, we had two swimming pools, 2 hot tubs, 2 club houses, one big and one smaller. When we first moved into Adobe Wells they had about 12 tables of Bridge. Both men and women played one night a week. The ladies played on Monday afternoons.

We really enjoyed Adobe Wells. Everyone was friendly, We got acquainted pretty fast. Every Friday night we had Happy Hour. That was when they announced the winners of the golf games. They announced what was coming up, any Birthday's or Anniversary's.

One time Lloyd came home from Golf, mad as he could be. I asked him what the matter was. He said "That Son of a bitch". He said it three times. I kept asking what he had done. Finally he said they were walking home and the guy asked him if he was lost. He said "Hell no, I wasn't lost." However he was several blocks past our house. The other guy was so good to him and he walked him back home. Another instance of how wonderful the people were in Adobe Wells.

We still visited and went on trips with the Gaults. We were at their home one time and Bettye said, "Would you like to go see The Steamboat Arabia?" I had never heard of it. So we all went to see it. The story is – One day this young man went to a bar. He set beside an older man. The man said, "I only regret one thing. I never tried to find and the Ship that sank on the river back in the 1800's. It was a supply ship full of Merchandise being shipped up the river." The ship hit a broken log that had fallen and the log went into the boat and it sank. The young man thought about it and went home and told his Father and his Uncle. They decided to try to find it

They finally located the ship about 5 miles in a farmer's field. The river had changed. The Farmer agreed they could dig for the ship if they could fill the land back in shape before the time came to plant his crops. They agreed. They brought up a lot of the merchandise and put it on display. They had to do a lot of cleaning to do on the merchandise. A box full of nails were all stuck together and needed separated. Silk material was still in perfect condition. The threads on the clothes were all gone, the shoe laces on the shoes were all gone, dishes were all ok, the pickles and most of the canned goods was ok, they ate some pickles to check it out. It was really quite interesting. They brought up a lot of stuff and put it in storage to clean up and display later. They did get the hole filled up in time. They offered the farmer a percentage of any profits they made, but he refused.

The first time we went to see the Steamship Arabia there was so much to still be done. All the people got off the ship when it sunk but a mule that was tied up in the front of the ship. About 4 years later we went through the ship museum again and they had so much more to show. If you go to Kansas City, be sure to go there.

We went to see the Titanic display when it was in Kansas City.

They traveled all around with the display. When you first go in the display they pin a name on your shoulder. They had brought up some of the stuff from the ship. At the end of the tour a person told you if you survived or not. Our names that they pined on our shoulder all survived but Tom. He was one of the men that gave up any chance of getting off to save others. Lloyd's name was wealthy. He was shipping brand new Rolls to America. He lived but his car didn't make it.

Pat and Gary O'Hare came down to visit with us from The Lake of the Ozarks. We were in McAllen for the winter. We took them to the Ebones Fairy. It is the last hand pulled Fairy still used for crossing a river into a foreign country. It took about four men to pull it across the Rio Grande River. They pulled on a big rope.

When you get to the other side you are in Mexico. They charged us going across and then coming back, it was only a dollar each. We walked on the boat but cars traveled back and forth all the time on the hand pulled boat.

Mexican people decorate the Cemetery's. They decorate everywhere with flowers, the Graves, the tombstones, and the fences around the Grave yard. Actually it is quite pretty. In one corner was the burn pile. The cemetery we were in rents the graves, if you do not pay the rent for the grave; they take the body up and burn the bones. Then they rent the grave again. We only went to one cemetery in Mexico so I don't know if all of them do it this way. We went in about 1950.

After we lived in Adobe Wells a couple of years, no one would take on "Entertainment Chairman" So I did. I really got into the job and was lucky enough to really get good Entertainers.

Claud and I went to Luby's to eat dinner. While we were there, the High School Choir came in, they walked around everyone singing while the people were eating and stopped just up from us to eat their dinner. I went over and talked with the man in charge of the Choir, Mr. Tanner.

I asked him if they ever entertained at the different Mobile Parks. He said no but he was willing. So I asked him if they could come and sing at Adobe Wells. He said to call him at school tomorrow and we would set up something. I called him the next day and we set a date. After that they came to Adobe Wells every year and entertained. They were really good singers.

Mr. Tanner said they were so thankful that I had stopped and talked with him. It was the beginning of a great Friendship with Mr. Tanner and a great start for the kids. They started entertaining all over the city at the different parks. Every one gave them a free will offering. They made enough money that once a year; they went some place as a group. That first year they went to New York. One of the girls in the choir interviewed for a singing position with a group in New York and she was hired to be in a play.

Mr. Tanner got so involved with the growth of the group that he had to turn the reservations over to his wife. She always called me first to set the date we wanted then signed up the other Parks. Mr. Tanner and the kids put on a big play at the school everyone year. Claud and I always went to the plays. I really liked it when they put on Oklahoma. It was my favorite play. Every student was so good. The kids had to try out for the privilege of singing with the group. They had to keep up their grades. The year that I moved to Frisco, Mr. Tanner retired. But I hear he still comes when they return to Adobe Wells. I would have them come when we had Pot Luck Dinners. I always told them to bring enough food for the kids. They got to eat theirs after the show.

I got a lot of good entertainers to come to our Happy Hour on Friday evening. We had the Sweet Adeline's several times, several groups of singers, Dancers, etc. One girl came down from Branson. She had a show there but less of a crowd in the winter so they came down and entertained us in McAllen. I got real well acquainted with her. The next time we went to our condo in Branson, She was entertaining there. I slipped down the stairs and waited for her at the bottom of the stairs. I was talking to her husband and she came down. She saw me and said "What in the world are you doing here?" to me and said up to me and said,

"What in the world are you doing in Branson?" We sit and talked for a while. Later I heard that she had a heart aneurism and died. It was so sad because she was only about 50.

We went to visit Vera and her family in Texas City, Texas. We had a great visit. She asked us that evening if we could drink a little wine with them. We said sure. She brought in a beer mug full of wine. I said I can not drink all of that. She said just sip as much as you want. We all drank it before we went to bed.

Lloyd went to bed at eleven, the rest of us stayed up and visited until about midnight. Lloyd was a sleep when I got in bed. I woke up at three AM and Lloyd was not in bed. At first I didn't worry because he was probably at the bathroom. He didn't come back so I go up and went through the house, then checked the yard. I woke Vera and Ben up and told them Lloyd was gone! I got dressed, got in the car to check around the neighborhood to see if I could find him. I told Vera to call the police. As I was backing out she called And said the police have him. We got in the car and went to get him. He had walked 8 blocks in the cold with just a night gown on. No shoes or coat. He was freezing. We got him home and washed his feet with luke warm water and he hollered, that's hot. I finally I got in the shower with him and rubbed him down with warm water. We went back to bed. He woke up the next morning and didn't even remember any of it. He was putting on his shoes and said, "My foot hurts; I must have stepped on something."

I went to my heart Doctor in McAllen. He found that I had a heart aneurism. The Doctor was scared for me. He said it was blooming out every breath I took. If it broke, I would be dead. The heart Specialist operated in two weeks. He told me it was very serious because any time you cut into the heart, it had a mind of its own. He had to patch it from the inside.

So I needed to get my affairs in order just in case, but he was very good so I didn't need to worry. I told him I was not worried, if it was my time to die I could do that but I was not in any hurry. I came through the operation good. So good in fact that they asked if they could put me in the regular hospital because others were worse off than me. He came in later and asked if I was getting good care. I said yes. He asked if the nurses were coming when I called. I said no, but that was alright. He left and then came back and had me moved right by the nurse station. He said do not push the button, just call out for them.

I played bridge a lot in Laurie. A couple came to bridge one day that had never played any bridge. It was miserable for everyone. The next week they came again. Everyone said some one teach them to play if they are going to keep coming each week. So I told them to come to my house and I would teach them to play. About 8 came. That was the beginning of my teaching bridge. I figured that I have taught over 200 people to play bridge. At Laurie, Adobe Wells in McAllen and Frisco, Texas. I am still teaching.

July 4th has always been a good holiday for my Family. We always got together on July 4th while we lived at the Lake of the Ozarks... Danny's parents came each year so they could visit with Danny too. One year, Ruth & Chester helped me serve the family a surprise dinner. They would order off a menu that was in Italian. Most people didn't know what they were ordering. You would have four courses; put three items on each course. Turn it in to us and we would serve what you ordered. The menu was bread, salad, knife, fork, spoon, water, toothpick, Lasagna, cake, coffee, napkin and soup. The fun part is that you can only eat whatever you ordered for each course. Like you might have to eat with your fingers or just drink your soup. Our friends thought it was fun.

Erik, Polly's son, had been sick but was feeling better when they came from Nebraska. I think he wasn't quite as well as we thought and gave it to Jim and Jimmy because they all slept in the same bedroom. Even Erik said he had been sick like that and was glad to be over it. But everyone blamed me for poisoning them. Everyone ended up sick but 5 of us, and we did all eat the same thing. It's a mystery but they all liked the idea that I poisoned them. I did really feel bad because Danny's folks never did come back to our house.

My cousin, Donna March, was attending a Church camp on the other side of the lake. She called me and asked if I could come and get her so she could see our place. I told her I would come and get her in the boat. She came and brought several friends. They had lunch with me and then I took them back to the camp.

One the way back to my house I felt a tight feeling across my back. I thought I was holding the steering wheel to tight. So I tried to relax. Two of those big cigar boats passed me racing with one on each side of me. They really rocked my boat. Finally I got home and did a perfect landing that is hard to do with a pontoon. [God was with me.] I went into the big cabin and lay down on the couch. Then I thought no one knows I am down here, I better get to the house. I made it to the house, stumbled to the living room couch and threw up all over the new carpet. Peggy was home and ran to the phone and called 911.

The Ambulance came and the two men talked and discussed if I was having a heart attack or just had indigestion. When we got to the hospital the heart attack was over but they kept me a couple more days any way. That was in October. Then I had another smaller heart attack in November. I was fixing Thanksgiving dinner and had to go rest. I told the family that it was just like the other heart attack but it didn't hurt as bad. The Doctor said the first heart attack killed most of the artery with blockage, and the second heart attack finished it.

Lloyd always had a garden. One year the Squirrels kept getting in his garden and eating the vegetables. Lloyd put an electrical fence around the garden. It was just one wire. A couple of nights later it rained and a squirrel touched the fence and it killed the squirrel. Lloyd let the squirrel lay on the ground for three days, and then he buried the squirrel. He took the fence down and put it away. There was never a squirrel in his garden again. It is amazing to me that squirrels learned to not go near the garden after seeing the other squirrel die.

While living at the lake we also had trouble with the squirrels eating our electrical wires that ran the little cart up and down the hill. This one stumped Lloyd he tried several things that did not work. One day he noticed his garden hose lying by the trolley. He cut the ends off and ran the electrical wires through the hose. They never bothered the wires again.

We lived at the lake for fifteen years. All the kids loved to come and see us. I did not work there. I asked some of the Realtors approximately how much they made and it didn't seem worth the hassle of lake roads to be working.

I played Bridge, taught bridge, and played golf. Lloyd and I played golf together some times.

Every time we had the kids home we always played poker. Lloyd wouldn't play anything else so we all played poker. I tried to keep it penny ante but if I wasn't playing they raised it to nickel, dine and quarter.

One time I was watching Lloyd comb his hair. He very carefully combed it straight back, then he pressed the waves back in place. He didn't know I was watching. His hair was so pretty, blond and lots of waves.

I enjoyed all our company that we had while living at the Lake. We all enjoyed the lake.

The third year as we were getting ready to go to McAllen for the winter, Lloyd yelled real loud. I ran in and asked what the matter was. He said he had a real bad pain in his stomach. I asked if he wanted to go to the Doctor. He said no, he would go when he got to McAllen. I called and made an appointment for him three days after we got to McAllen.

The Doctor checked him over and put him right in the hospital. He had tests and they found he was full of cancer of the pancreas.

When they found the cancer, I called the kids. Carol and Polly came down to be with us.

They operated and tried to clear his passages for elimination so he wouldn't be in pain. He was brought into the recovery room. The male nurse told us that we should just talk to him like he could hear what we were saying. We were talking to him and each other when Carol said, "Mom do you think Daddy can hear us, do you think he knows we are here?" Lloyd answered "I know". That is all he ever said in his life. I asked if he was going to make it through this. The Doctor said no, he was only alive & breathing on the oxygen.

I went home that night and called all the kids again. They all said for me to do what I had to do. So I got his living will out not to be kept alive artificially and gave it to the Doctor the next morning. That was the hardest thing I have ever had to do in my life. They notified me the next morning he had died.

Lloyd died at 2 AM. He died Christmas morning December 25, 1996. We had been married 48 1/2 years. He was 70 years old. The last years were the best in a long time. We did love each other. He wouldn't be coming home for any more weekends.

Carol and Peggy were there just before he died, and for the funeral. Thank God I wasn't home by myself.

Now I had another problem. I was in charge of the Christmas program at the Club house. I was in the program. What do I do? I asked the girls,

"What should I do?" They said do what you want to do. I said, "I don't know what I want to do. If I go ahead with the program, will people think that I didn't love Lloyd?" Finally I said, "We have nothing here for your Christmas dinner so we will go to the club house." We did the program.

After the program, Bob said the blessing for dinner. He ended it with, "God please help Twylia and her family after loosing her husband this morning." The whole room gasped. Most of them did not know he had died yet.

We had the Memorial Service at the Club House. Most of the residents were there. A lot of the Friends stood up and told memories of him. Later they served refreshments. Lloyd loved to play golf. Even at his worst he knew the way to our golf course and would play with anyone that happened to be there. They were all so good to him.

*Lloyd James Adams born: 5/16/1926. He died 12/25/1996. We had been married 48 years and 7 months. He died at age 70 in McAllen, Texas. He is buried in Fredonia. We have a double tombstone for both of us.

I had his body prepared in McAllen and then had it sent to Fredonia for the funeral. The Funeral home in Fredonia picked up the body in Kansas City. Julia, Charles' wife, made all the arrangements in Fredonia. The funeral in the church, the dinner for everyone, the 21 gun salute, many good friends came to the funeral and the burial. All I asked was that it not be depressing. Everyone told funny and good memories.

After Lloyd died I could not keep the home at the Lake. It was too big and just too much for me to take care of by myself. I put it on the market to sell. I finally got a full price offer if I could carry part of it back as a second loan. I told them I would accept their offer. My son said I should not carry the 2nd loan. I might not get it paid to me. The Bank had their 1st mortgage and I only had the 2nd loan. I figured if I don't get it at least it is sold and I won't have to worry about it. They did pay every penny to me.

After Lloyd died I had to down size and get rid of a lot of stuff. I sold my wonderful home on the 10 mile lake marker. I asked the kids what I had that they would like to have. I gave Carol my dining room, table, chairs and china closet. I gave her the dishes that Lloyd had bought in Japan. Jim and Jerry said nothing but some of the big old money that Grandma had given me. Dexter wanted the tools that I would not be using. Polly was in Nebraska and didn't know what she would want. Later I gave her a nice big diamond ring. Peggy chose the Bedroom set but didn't need it or have a place for it right then, I had to down size to move into a little mobile home, so Carol ended up with the bedroom set. I promised Peggy my 25th Anniversary ring that Lloyd had given me. So I hope everyone was happy with what they had at the end.

I loved Lloyd and missed him. I even began to realize that Lloyd was a lot like his Mother. Neither of them showed much affection. She would give us a duty hug when we arrived for a visit. He did love me and that is what was important.

Lloyd was a strong man, an intelligent man, he was a born leader. Sometimes pretty vain, sometimes he was pretty selfish. I loved him. I missed him. I knew he would not be home on weekends ever again.

Each year I still went to McAllen for the winter. I loved my little gray house. It had windows on three sides in the living room. I was looking straight at the Adobe Wells Club House.

We played bridge one night a week at the club house. I can't remember the night but I think it was on a Wednesday. We usually had about 10 or 12 tables both men and women that played. It was a fun night.

I belonged to a two table bridge group and we played on Monday afternoon. Sue, Delores, Helen, Betty, B.J., Ruth, Mary Jane and me. It was all girls, we took turns playing at each others homes. Cora played if she was in Adobe Wells. Bridge has played a big part in my life.

I kept going to McAllen after Lloyd died because we already owned the house. I was very lucky and happy to say I had made a lot of good friends. They all pitched in to help if I needed something and still included me in all the visits and parties. Most of our life Lloyd had to travel, my good friends were always there to help me.

Oliver called me in McAllen and asked me if I had any plans. I said yes, I am going to Alaska. Now I had not thought of going to Alaska. But Lloyd and I had talked about going to Alaska before he died. We talked about going on our 50th Wedding Anniversary. Oliver asked me who was going with me. I said "I thought you might want to go." He did, so I told him to make the plans and I would just pay half.

He made the plans, on July 9, 1997 we flew to Anchorage, Alaska. The next morning we flew to Kotzebue, Alaska. This is like you see in the movies. It is an old weather worn town. We took a bus tour of the town.

The guide stopped the bus; we all got out, and pulled up some moss. He squeezed the moss and water came out of it. He passed the moss to each of us on the bus. Oliver and I were the last ones and the water still came out. We were right across from Russia. On the map, it looked real close, about 5 miles.

The way they used to stake a claim in Alaska to pan for gold is stand up and hold your arm straight out holding a hoe, someone else measures straight down from the end of the hoe and marks the spot. Then do the same thing with your other arm and mark the spot. That is your claim and no one else can pan on your claim. I asked him if anyone still panned for the gold. He said yes. Teachers liked to come and pan for gold. They came the months that there was no school. They found enough gold to make the trip worthwhile.

I asked him what the telephone poles were doing on the ground. He said they were not telephone poles. They were trees. It is only about a foot to ice under the tundra. When the roots of the tree hit the ice they spread apart and the tree falls. The roots are too short to hold the tree up.

We went on to Nome, Alaska the next day. They were getting ready for the big dog race. A man had the dog sleds all ready for us to see how they work. The lead dog is all business. You cannot touch him or talk to him. You can pet the other dogs but not the lead dog. He asked if anyone wanted to drive the dogs. I said yes, I do. So I drove the dogs about 30 feet. Then another man drove the team about the same distance.

The next morning we flew back to anchorage. We got a certificate showing we crossed the Arctic Circle, next we took a bus through the Denali Park, the Tundra Wildlife Tour. We saw several different animals a Mama Bear and three baby cubs, but they were big enough to keep up with their Mother.

We got on a river boat tour. We went on the Chena & Tanami Rivers. We saw a Chena Village, another dog sled, and Downtown Chicken, Alaska. It is a restaurant, and two toilets. That is all, no other buildings.

We got on a Yukon Queen cruse. It was a small but nice ship. We went by the Alaska Pipeline Terminus Valdez. We went to Klondike Kate's Restaurant in Dawson City, on to the Gaslight Follies and the Palace Grand Theatre. It was close to the time of the USA Beauty contest. Five girls representing their towns were on the ship; they wore their native costumes and told us about their life.

We panned for gold several times. We got on a train going through the White Pass summit, Dead horse gulch; this got its name because when the people tried to go up the mountain on a horse, or even lead them, the horses could not make the climb and would slip down and die. Some would make it but many could not. A mule was better to climb up the mountains.

When we got to Glacier Bay, Alaska we flew up on the glacier by Helicopters. Oliver scared me; he was walking all over on the ice. The ice was very slick to walk on. I was looking down in a crevasse it was the prettiest blue. I didn't get very close, I was a little uneasy on the ice.

We were on the Holland America Line ship. We stopped in Ketchikan, Alaska. We were headed back from our journey.

We docked in Vancouver, British Columbia. Then on to Seattle, Washington, we stopped in and visited Cecil and Frances Henley. We went up to the restaurant at the top of the Space Needle. We were there July 27, 1997. Cecil and Frances lives by Mt. Rainier. When we left Henley's we flew back to Kansas City. We left a car there so we had transportation back home. I really enjoyed Oliver and our trip together. We got close again after so many years apart.

Oliver's wife was Dorothy Maxine Lawson Dexter. Oliver and Dorothy got married 3/6/1948. Two months before Lloyd and I got married May 30, 1948.

Oliver lost Dorothy in August 1996. I lost Lloyd, December 25, 1996, on Christmas day. Dorothy died 4 months before Lloyd. I guess I just walked in Oliver's footsteps.

I had been going to McAllen, now for 3 winters and I had not met the girl down the street. One day she came out side in her yard. I dropped everything and went down and introduced myself. Her name was Tina, she was pretty short. I asked her if she played bridge, she said no. I asked if she played golf, she said no. I asked what she did. She said she was a painter. At one time she had taught painting but quit teaching when her husband died. I asked when he died. She said three years ago. I said three years! My husband has only been gone for three months. Others had tried to get her to come to happy hour on Fridays but she wouldn't go. I guess she related to me losing my husband because I asked her to go out to dinner with me and she agreed. From then on we were together most of the time.

One time while we were visiting at my house, she said she felt so sorry for her friend Claud. He just walks his little dog. He is so lonesome. She would tell me over and over. I finally said. "Why don't you invite him to go to happy hour with you?" She said, "No, people would think I was after him." His wife had just died with Parkinson's disease. She had not been able to do any thing for 3 years, and was confined to her bed for 2 years.

Tina would come up every morning and bring her coffee cup. I don't make coffee so she brought her own. She would read the paper while I ate my breakfast.

Violet called and told me about Mustang Island. It was not far but on the beach and might be fun. I told Tina about it and she wanted to go too. So the three of us spent a week on the Island. We swam, and played in the water. We went out to eat every day, but ate cerial and coffee for breakfast in the room. I was with two coffee addicts.

The next summer Tina came to Missouri to visit me. She said She would be at Springfield on June 4th at 10 AM. She called from her place in Oklahoma.

Peggy lived in Springfield so she went with me to pick Tina up. We were lucky because there were only three airlines in Springfield. We went to the first one and asked if a Tina Plummer was coming in on their airline at 10 AM from Oklahoma? NO. So we went to the next two airlines, NO. OK now what! We went to the first airline and asked if a Tina Plummer was coming in at all. NO. The last one said NO, but a Leona Plummer was coming in and the plane had already landed. I asked if everyone was off the plane, she said all but one little lady in a wheel chair. They came out as we were talking and it was Tina. I ran up to her and asked what was wrong. She jumped up and said nothing. She always traveled in a wheel chair. Then she didn't have to ever worry about connections.

We had a great visit. I introduced her to all my friends. Then it was time to take her back to the airport to go home. I told her the next time she wanted me to pick her up; she needed to tell me the airline, the flight number, the day and the time.

It was about a couple of months later when we were sitting on her porch and this man came by with his little dog. I had never seen him before. She called for him to come over and she would introduce him to her friend. It was Claud. She asked him if he would like to go out to dinner with us that evening. He said yes. We became a three some after that. Several weeks went by and one day he came over and knocked on my door. I said come in and where is Tina? He said, 'I didn't come to see Tina, I came to see you." I said, OK, come on in.

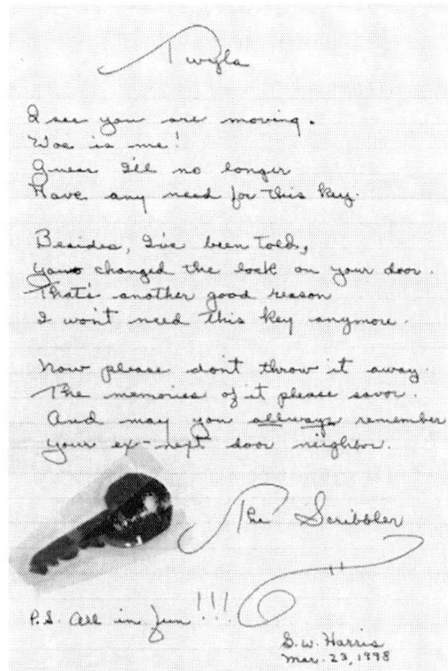

Twyla

I see you are moving.
Woe is me!
Guess I'll no longer
Have any need for this key.

Besides, I've been told,
You changed the lock on your door.
That's another good reason
I won't need this key anymore.

Now please don't throw it away.
The memories of it please savor.
And may you allways remember
your ex-next door neighbor.

The Scribbler

P.S. All in fun!!!

S.W. Harris
Mar. 23, 1998

That was the beginning of a wonderful courtship. He was so thoughtful, so kind, and he sure didn't waste time. He purposed after about three weeks of us going together. I told him that was too soon after his wife had died. He said they had been married for 53 years. But he hadn't had a wife for 4 years. He was ready to get married. We set the date as March 14, 1998.

He wrote me a cute story; I saved it in our Wedding book. At our next Friday regular meeting, the Master of Ceremony's called some of the men up to the front of the room. He asked them to leave all the keys that they had to my house on the table. Claud didn't want any of those men having any of my keys. About 7 men brought up keys.......It got a good laugh.

Claud and I got married on March 14, 1998, at the St. Marks Methodist Church. Tina was my Brides Maid, and Carol stood up with me. Claud had his son, Kenneth DuBois as his best man. It was a lovely church wedding. Peggy, my youngest daughter, and Maxine, Claud's daughter, were with us too.

Rev. Ricky Sanderford was the minister that married us. He was the Pastor of the First Methodist Church.

After the wedding we took the wedding party out to eat. Then we went to the Adobe Wells Club house for the reception. I think almost every one in Adobe Wells attended. Several of our Relatives, Sunday school and Church friends came to the wedding. Just about every one we knew.

Claud had lived there for a long time and knew everybody. We bought six boxes of wine. We had a beautiful 3 tiered, double layered cake. We had 5 double layered cakes around the big wedding cake. All was eaten but the top and the biggest bottom layer.

We saved the small top layer and ate it to celebrate our one year Anniversary together.

My cousin's Virginia Dedrickson and Wanda Wilke came to our wedding. They were Daddy's sister Trilla's girls. They were living in McAllen at that time. The next year they moved back to Truman, Minnesota area.

About a week after the wedding, we were invited to Paul & Betty Martens to go out to dinner with them. They served every body a drink. I am not a big or fast drinker, so I was just sipping my drink. Paul said "Hurry up Twyla, we need to go. "Then he said, just bring it with you. We got in their car and he drove right to the back of our house. There was a group of friends behind our house and in the Neighbors drive way. They had Claud and Me get in a golf trailer where they had put two lawn chairs. We had quite a parade. There were about thirty friends walking behind us. Every one came out to clap and throw rice at us as we passed. They drove up and down Adobe Wells streets banging on pie tins. It was a laud Shivaree, but it was a lot of fun.

After the parade we went back to the Neighbors house where they had a Keg of beer. The men told Claud he had to pay for the beer. Claud started to get his bill fold out and they said NO, it's already paid for. They were just teasing him.

They had plenty of food laid out on our back porch. They said they were going to short sheet the bed but the house was locked. Later we realized that the back porch door was not locked. They didn't check there.

I called each of the kids and told them about the Shivaree and not a one knew what I was talking about except Peggy. She said I had told her about a couple while I was in High School and we had a shivaree for them. The couple climbed up in a tree trying to hide from us. The Guys found them and he had to push the bride around in a Wheel borrow. Later they passed out cigars for the men and candy bars for the ladies.

I had already sold the lake house in Laurie. I had bought a small mobile home to live in before I went back for the winter in Adobe Wells. The small mobile home was on Carefree Lane in Laurie, Missouri. When Claud and I got married we added a big porch and an office to my house. Claud wanted a car port so we added that. This is a picture of our house in Laurie. It turned into a cute little house.

One day I had some tomato plants to put out. Claud tried for some time to plant them and he couldn't ever dig a hole. There were too many rocks. I went to the office and asked the owner if I could have the left over blocks that were left when they pulled a different mobile house away. He said yes, use as many as you need. Claud and I built a garden. We put in new dirt and Claud planted me my tomatoes and some cantaloupes in the garden. Our garden was producing tomatoes and some cantaloupes. We got to enjoy a few but it was time for us to return to McAllen. We told the neighbors to help themselves while we were gone. Just clean out the garden when it quit producing.

Claud and I went every year to see all the Kids. It was real good for us to go see Maxine, his daughter. Claud had not been to see her and her family for over four years, because his wife had been sick with Parkinson's. Maxine had four girls, and each girl had 3 children. We always had a good visit with them. It was always a two or three week trip to see everybody.

Palace View - Branson, MO - Claud & Twylia

Every two years the Clinesmith Family has a big Reunion. It is held either at Buffalo, or Fredonia, Kansas. They always planned a fun time on Saturday, then a good visit with everyone and a good dinner on Sunday. One year we went on a hay wagon to the Great Grandparents Homestead Farm. [George and Mary Clinesmith] We also went to the old School House where most of us had gone to school. It had eight grades in one room, a wood burning stove, and we all had to take our lunch. It was a fun trip with good old memories for everyone.

One year we had a big Shrimp boil, One year they fixed Bar-B-Q Calf in a big pit. Calvin and Rena had this at their home. You never know for sure what they are going to do. The best part is the next generation has taken over now. It is always the last Saturday and Sunday in July.

I always take my Family Tree Book. They all like to read about the Relatives and their own family. Every year someone seems to be writing something from the Book.

This is a picture of our home in Adobe Wells. It was a very comfortable home. Three bedrooms two baths. We added a new porch, now we can sit on the porch and visit with the people going by. Our address was 4901 Daffodil, #166, McAllen, Texas.

Claud and I did a lot of traveling. We went to Hawaii two times. The first time we went to visit Tim and Janice Monro. Janice was born in Hawaii, she was a native Hawaiian. Janice and Tim saved this one pineapple for me to pick. You put your hands on both sides of the pineapple and twist it and it will come off in your hands.

Claud and Tim worked together when Claud was living in Hawaii. Claud lived in Hawaii for 12 years working for the Oil Company. They loved living in Hawaii but it was too far from all the Family.

The Japanese attacked Pearl Harbor in Hawaii in 1941, it was 71 years ago. They sank the USS Arizona in the Harbor. The ship was full of their crew and all were lost and still in the ship.

Claud told me that when they were trying to raise money for the USS Arizona Memorial, Elvis Presley gave a program and donated all the money he made to the Memorial fund. It was not known to the general public, but the Hawaii people all thought he was a wonderful and generous man.

The Monro's lived on the Big Island of Hawaii. They met us at the air port in complete costume. They put a lay on both of us and insisted we go to their home for a few days. We had already rented a Hotel room and car, but it was so good of them to take us. They knew where they were going, so we saw twice as much. Each day they took us in a different direction and showed us every thing.

One time we were looking at a blocked road where the Volcano had erupted and flowed over the road. Someone had laid a big leaf down and it had been full of sea water. The water had dissolved and there was only salt in the leaf. Little things like this really interest me. It is something you just don't think about.

We went to a big swimming pool beside the ocean, the waves washed into the pool. By the edge of the pool, the water was cool, but toward the back of the pool, the water was pretty hot. It was the volcano under ground that heated it. The pool had no floor. So you had to be careful, one place was flat, and then a big stone, you never knew. I swam with my feet up so I didn't touch the floor most of the time.

We were there on King Kamehameha' Birthday. This was celebrated by the Natives. Janice was born in Hawaii so we were included. They had a big parade; we followed them to the park.

There was food all down the street. It was mostly sea food; the Hawaiian's all usually ate sea food. We didn't see any thing we wanted to eat until we got completely to the end of the line. They had hamburgers so we all got hamburgers. We went inside the pavilion and looked at the Historical things on display. There was a Tattoo man there and girls lined up to have their hips tattooed. They were putting their Ancestors name put on their hips.

We went outside to watch the dancers. It started with the young boys doing the hula, then the young girls, then the older boys, then the older girls, working their way to the adults. The Men used to be the only ones that danced. Kind of like the American Indians, it started with only the men dancing.

One of the things I really liked in Hawaii was the fresh pineapple. It was so good and full of sweet juice. The Restaurants all served pineapple on every plate of food that they served.

I was so surprised several years later that Dole sold all of their pineapple orchards in Hawaii. The Hawaiian's only raised enough for the residents to eat. Dole was a big loss to Hawaii, they had grown the pineapple for many years.

This was Christmas at Kelly's home Several years ago. She and Sean invited Carol & Danny, Claud & Me, Sean's parents, Bruce and Sousan Souri.

It was a real nice Christmas with the little kids, Noah and Sophia got most of the attention, and presents. This was Claud's last Christmas with the family.

I decided to sell my house in Laurie. When Claud and I got married, we decided to just live in Adobe Wells. Claud lived in McAllen for a lot of years before I even met him. We stayed the rest of the summer in Laurie. Then moved everything left to Adobe Wells. I had already sold my little mobile home in Adobe Wells when Claud and I got married. So now we went from owning three houses to one. Claud was such a wonderful man.

Ken Mausley was one of neighbors in Adobe Wells. Several of the neighbors got together and we had an 85th birthday party for him. We gave him a beautiful white birthday cake to cut and serve. He tried several times to cut it. He couldn't get it to cut. He finally told the hostess to cut it for him. We all laughed and she brought a different cake in to be served. She had decorated a sponge cake first. The expression on his face when he could not cut the cake was so funny. It was a good joke.

Shortly after Claud and I got married Claud got the itch for a new car. He said he had always wanted a Lincoln. So we sold his car, and my car and bought a Lincoln. About every two years he got that car itch. After four new cars when he got the itch again, I said no, I don't want a new car. I like this one. It was a 2006 Chrysler. Everything worked good. We did not need a new car. Finally I told him to go ahead and buy a new car and I would keep the old one. He decided we could wait a little while but the warranty had expired. Later Claud died and I felt so guilty about not buying his new car. I am still driving my Chrysler. Danny put new tires, new windshield wipers, filled it with gas, changed the oil and that old car runs like new. It also looks great.

Howard and Delores Armentrout went with Claud and me to Big Bend, Texas. It is a mountain area with beautiful streams. The water in the streams was so clear and fresh. If it were not so cold, I would have loved to go wading.

We went through an old Army base. It was called Fort Davis, it was not used anymore. It is now just a tourist attraction. The men started walking around and looking at the parade grounds. I noticed a little truck golf cart. I asked the man if we could use it to drive around. He said sure, go ahead. So Delores and I rode all around the base.

We went by a few of the homes where the families used to live. They didn't have many left for us to see, it was now just a tourist attraction. Also the officer's quarters, and the barracks where the men lived. The huge area in the middle was for training and marching. We drove all around and saw it all.

When we got back Claud and Howard were watching a movie that was set up to watch the training and etc. That is when we offered the men the truck to drive around too. They said no, they were ready to go.

As we were coming home we came to Sonora, Texas. They had a big cave there. The sign on top of the door said it was so many feet down. Now I don't have any trouble going down so we all decided to go on through the cave. I am so glad we did because there was a big ice dripping area that looked just like a bunch of Butterflies. It was beautiful. I had never seen drippings that looked like butterflies before. That made the whole trip worthwhile.

It was time to start back up the stairs. I managed just fine for a while, then I started getting tired and out of breath. So I called a rest time. Then we started again, I called another rest time. The third time the young girl in front of me stuck out her arm and said hang on, I am not a bit tired, and I run every day. I hung on or I would never have made it to the top. [I have asthma and sometimes I get out of breath.] When we got to the top I looked over at Howard and he looked worse than me. His face was red as a beet. He was breathing real hard. We all set down and rested before we started to the car. I am glad we did go and we got to see the beautiful butterflies. I worried about Howard, but we all rested for a while and made it OK. One of my favorite trips was going to the Panama Canal. Several of our friends in Adobe Wells said they would like to go while it still belonged to the United States. I told Oliver and Shirley we were planning to go. Oliver asked if they could go too. I told them sure, all it takes is money. There were 82 of us going together from Adobe Wells.

We went through several other places on the way. One was Curacao. We woke up that morning, I got up and looked out our balcony door. The seen was beautiful. I said, "Wake up Claud, You have to see this." Most of the Islands were pretty drab. This one was pretty, all different colors. We got a guide to show us the town. I told him I really thought the town was pretty. He said their Mayor told all the residents to paint their property a pretty color. They all painted everything one color. The house blue, the fence blue, everything you can paint the same color.

Then we came to the Panama Canal. The QE2 was just starting through the canal. After they got a good start, we started through. There were two canals with a small area between the two ships. When the QE2 was up, we were down, when we were up, they were down. We started waving and hollering at each other when we passed the other ship. The Qe2 got out first and headed to Acapulco. They were first and we had to wait until they left. They were on a world tour. While we waited we tossed coins in the water for the native boys to catch them. I didn't know that if you tossed a quarter in the water it fell flat and waved back and forth and the boys had plenty of time to catch the coins. I learn a lot on most of our trips. This is a picture of our group that went on the trip.

Claud knew that I liked to play bridge. One day out of the blue before we were married he told me he played bridge. I was so glad to hear that, I could not get Lloyd to even think of playing. We got married and I invited a couple over to play bridge. After they went home, Claud said he needed to talk to me. He said "If you never ask me to play bridge again, I promise that I will never say anything, no matter how much you play." I answered, "That's a deal!"

Sue Johnson - Dick Hopper

We have wonderful friends in Adobe Wells. This is Sue Johnson and Dick Hopper. They are not married but they have lived together several years.

B.J. called me every morning after Claud died. She would say are you all right? I'd say yes. B.J. was a good bridge player too. She was appreciated so much. About a year later she got sick and just laid around in bed. I tried to help her but she just kept saying she was all right. I moved to Dallas to be with the girls. She never told me what was wrong but later she died of cancer. After B.J., died Jim moved to Huston to their daughters. Later I heard that he had died too.

Mary Jane and Swede Wogsland are from Rushville,Indiana. Mary Jane was a great cook and they had us over for dinner and visiting many times. Claud and I went to visit them in Indiana once. They had a nice home with a great big yard. Mary Jane was still in Adobe Wells a year after I moved to Frisco to be near my kids. Then they sold their place in Adobe Wells too. Swede died a few years after they moved back to their home. Mary Jane and I still keep in touch by phone.

Betty and Wayne Stewart were from Minot, North Dakota. They were great friends, of Course Betty was in my bridge group. I just could not tell you who was the best cook of all the girls. They were all great. We had many get togethers, some times just a couple and other times all of us together. Wayne and Betty sold their home in Adobe Wells shortly after the rest of us did and moved back to North Dakota. Wayne celebrated his 90th birthday this year. They lived on the golf course. Everyone in Adobe Wells loved golf. Betty and Wayne are both still with us. They are the only couple left of my best friends there.

We also had long time Friends, Tom and Bettye Gault, Marshall and Elizabeth Lett, Lou and Frank Belcher, Betty and Harry Brunk. I am so blessed to have wonderful friends.

I have had the opportunity to go on many trips. Some were with Lloyd and some were with Claud. Oliver and I had a nice trip to Alaska. This was between our marriages.

Oliver married Shirley Feb. 14, 1998 in Dallas. I married Claud just a month later, March 14, 1998.

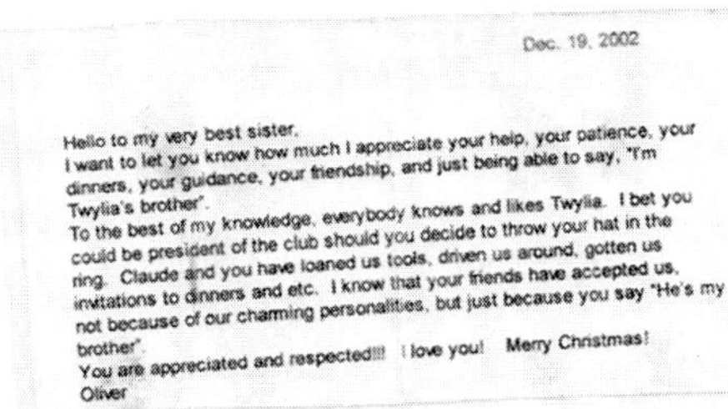

Dec. 19, 2002

Hello to my very best sister,
I want to let you know how much I appreciate your help, your patience, your dinners, your guidance, your friendship, and just being able to say, "I'm Twylia's brother".
To the best of my knowledge, everybody knows and likes Twylia. I bet you could be president of the club should you decide to throw your hat in the ring. Claude and you have loaned us tools, driven us around, gotten us invitations to dinners and etc. I know that your friends have accepted us, not because of our charming personalities, but just because you say "He's my brother".
You are appreciated and respected!!! I love you! Merry Christmas!
Oliver

I guess I just copied him all along. We were both very happy with our new mates. Oliver and Shirley came down to visit with us in McAllen. We got along so well together that they decided to move down and buy a mobile home. They were at McAllen for two years. They were just talking about buying a bigger mobile home.

Oliver and I played a game of golf about every morning. Oliver wrote me this note after they moved down to Adobe Wells. One morning he called and said he was tired and did not feel up to a game of golf that day. Two more days he called, on the third day he called and said he was going back to Dallas to his regular Doctor. Oliver wrote this note to me just before he returned to Dallas to see his Doctor.

We were going on our regular trip to see all the kids. We stopped in at Carol and Danny's first. She had a big dinner and invited Oliver and Shirley to join us. He began to look tired. I told him to go on home, I didn't want him to get to tired visiting.

He said, "I will stay 30 more minutes," Then they were leaving and I pulled him close and told him I loved him. I stepped back and he pulled me back down and he said "I love you too."

The next morning Cindy called and said Oliver was in the hospital. Claud and I hurried to the hospital. Cindy told me where they had taken him. I ran to that room and three Doctors were giving him chest pressure trying to bring him back to life. He was already gone. We stayed in Dallas for his funeral.

Delores and Howard Armentrout went with Claud and me to Hawaii. They had never been there before. We took a Helicopter ride. We went down inside a volcano. Hawaii is so pretty and so many beautiful flowers. We were getting ready to go home the next day, we had been there a week. While we were just riding around looking at the scenery, we were right beside the ocean. I said stop. Claud stopped; I got out and walked to the water, took my shoes off and waded in the ocean. I just could not go to the ocean and not even get wet. The others did not even get wet. They enjoyed seeing Hawaii so I guess they did have a good time.

Cora, John Coventon, Claud and I went on a trip together in Europe. We cruised down the Great Rivers of Europe from Amsterdam to Vienna. There were many giant castles, and grape vineyards.

One of the first things that we were told was do not walk in the bicycle path. They all ride bicycles and they go fast. They will not stop for you. There was a separate lane for the cars and if you are walking you better watch the traffic.

Amsterdam is quite interesting. They have a lot of canals right in town; the boats that people live in are on the canals. Claud asked, "With so many people living on the canals, how you keep the water sanitary?" They open the gates at each end of town each night. Then the water flows downstream all night, so by day time the water is clean again. The next day we continued our river cruise and we saw children playing in the water, downstream! I hope they were far enough downstream for them to be ok.

We decided to get on the train that goes around the city to get an idea of what is there all at once. The first thing we did wrong was to get in the train in the front. The man driving was nice and told us to pay in the back. So we went clear to the back, paid and sit down. Later a group of boys started to get on the train in the front, the driver hollered at them to go to the back; he said you know better than that.

I turned around and asked the money man if we passed something important to let us know. He said, "I am not a tour guide." I said, "Oh, I am sorry." Just a few minutes later he started telling us everything that we passed. He also told us that his son was in college in California. They go see him a couple of times a year.

Sitting just in front of us was a man that had a lot of Tattoos. He had them everywhere. Where there was a spot free, he had piercing. He had them on his eyebrows, his lips, his nose, even his tongue, all around his ears, everywhere. I cannot imagine anyone hiring that man to work for them.

Amsterdam is the chief city and Capital. In the 1500's they were ruled by the Spanish, then in 1795 the French took them over, the French rule lasted until 1815. Then the United Kingdom of the Netherlands was established and it has been the Netherlands ever since.

Amsterdam is an open city; I guess that means you can do most anything. The Ladies of the night are hanging out their windows inviting the men in to visit. Cora and I both hung on to our men!

We went through a Diamond business. There are no perfect diamonds. They sent up 3 different grades of diamonds for me to see. I was very interested in the diamonds. A good one caret diamond was between $6.000 to 12,000. No, I didn't buy one but I was so interested that Claud began to worry.

One story they told us was about two brothers. They built their castles right beside each other. Then they had a fallen out when one brother married the other brother's girlfriend. They built a big wall between them. I hope they eventually made up. Life is too short for families to break up permanently.

We went through 66 locks going down the rivers. The last two were 80 feet deep. This is one of the locks. Ships need to go through a lock to get to water higher or lower. When they go through the lock the water will be the level to go on wherever they want to go. I found it quite interesting to see the different heights of the water. Claud enjoyed this trip more than any of the others. He liked to just sit, relax and look at the scenery as you travel down the river.

One of the bridges that we went under was really a close call. They filled the bilge with water to lower the boat so we could make it under the bridge. They laid down all the furniture, lowered the Captains scope, and told all passengers to go down stairs.

I was on the steps going down with my camera and took a picture of us going under the bridge.

There was a Lady on the ship from the United States that went to College in Europe. While we were going down one of the rivers a group ridding bicycles met us at a lock. This group had gone to college with her. She had written to them and told them she would be on our ship. They were on the bank as we were going through the lock. They talked back and forth, then went to the next place Where they could be by the ship and they could talk. At the end of their visit, they all sang their old school song. It was so touching that I cried then and now telling you about it.

We were in some town during the River trip, Cora wanted some lace curtains. At each town they had a walking tour and they would show us the main part of town then we'd go back to the ship. Cora and I went back to town looking for her curtains. I looked at my watch and told her it was just about time to head back to the ship.

Cora said there is the river, we can just follow it. We walked a pretty long ways and didn't see the ship. I stopped another couple with badges like ours. They said we were going in the wrong direction. We didn't know that there were two rivers that met. We turned around and started back, this time to the ship.

It had not been very long since I was operated on for an aneurysm in the heart. It had to be patched from the inside. I was really getting tired by now, and I had to rest every little while. Finally we saw the ship.

Claud and John were waiting at the gang plank, they were worried too. They have a smart way of knowing if everyone was back on the ship. When you left the boat you put your key in a basket. When you get back on the boat you pick up your key. Cora and mine were the only keys left.

We came to a spot on the river where the water was higher than usual. They made everyone go down below and get off the deck. Then they lowered the ship by adding some water to the Bilge. I am not sure I am telling you this right but they lowered the ship so we could go under the bridge. I took a picture of us going under the bridge. To take the picture I had to lay down on the floor down a few steps. What I don't do to get a great picture.

Germany was interesting because of Hitler. Hitler built the Coliseum for offices. It was bigger than the one in Rome. They ran out of money. Hitler said, "Just go ahead and build the Coliseum and we will just take over another country." They never finished the Coliseum and Hitler lost the war.

We stood where Hitler gave his speeches to the people. We went through the court house where they tried Hitler. It was all interesting. We went through a big Museum in Germany. They had a big thick pocket watch. It was supposed to be one of the first pocket watches. They had a world map that did not have the North America Continent it. They had a picture of Rembrandt, it was a self-portrait of him. They said it was one of most popular pictures that people enjoyed seeing.

When we started to fly home we discovered the airplane was cancelled. They finally put us on a plane to Frankfort and we had to fly on First Class to Chicago, then on to St. Louis. I told Claud that I always wanted to go first class. Jim picked us up and we drove on home from his house. The next day the airline sent us our luggage, right to the house in Laurie, Missouri.

In Mexico we went to Copper Canyon, Every one told us that it was even bigger than the Grand Canyon. No, it was not. We were riding in a bus to Copper Canyon and stopped to eat. We went into this Restaurant. The bus driver suggested we order Enchiladas' with green sauce. They were so good, we stopped at the same place coming back home.

We went to Mazatlan in Mexico. We really liked Mazatlan, it had a beautiful beach. We talked about going back there again. But we never made it. As we were leaving the restaurant we saw a man painting. We stopped and watched for awhile. We both liked the painting so much, we bought it. It is hanging right now in my Hall.

Claud and I went to Cancun with Oliver and Shirley. They had a time share. We stopped at a place and we all tried on a big Mexican Sombrero. We did not buy one, but it made a good picture. If you have ever traveled on a time share you know you have to hear a big sales pitch.

There was a brand new time share just opening with Oliver's time share company. We all four went to see it. The floors were black marble. As we were walking along Claud fell down 4 steps. The steps were not marked in any way and you could not see them they were black and matched the floor. Claud was lucky; he rolled down the steps and was not hurt. It scared all of us. The salesman most of all, he just knew there would be a law suit.

Another time Oliver and Shirley met us in Pioneer Village in Nebraska. There were several big buildings. They had a lot of different things there. Old cars, doll collections, dishes, An Old Merry Go Round that still works. They had a lot of farm equipment, just all kinds of things.

Oliver and Shirley went on with us to Yellow Stone National Park. We shared a condo for a week. Our Oldsmobile was a car that had movies in the back seat. Shirley said that she got car sick in the back seat, so Oliver and I rode in the back and watched a movie. The next day we all went to the Yellow Stone National park. We saw the animals, and drove all through the park.

Carol & Danny went with us to a time share near San Diego that Lawrence Welk owned. I wanted to go to the San Diego Zoo to see the biggest Zoo in the United Sates. I was so disappointed, the St. Louis Zoo is better. They have a train in St. Louis that takes you all around the park. St. Louis also has several animal shows and San Diego only had a bird show. Once when we went to the St. Louis Zoo they had an Elephant show. The first big Elephant sit on a stool, the 2^{ndE}elephant put a bib around him, the 3rd elephant shaved the 1st Elephant. I will never forget that show. I do sound a little predicable bragging on St. Louis. One time they had a seal show, and they always had a Monkey Show.

We had a nice visit at Uncle Clair's Daughter's home in Newport Beach. Eden has had several names. When she was young her name was Iverna. She was once an actress, and then her name was Dixie Dexter. Next she had a business and her name was Eden when she was married to Evan Ryl. She gave motivational sales meetings; they were so successful that she began to make films. She made one called "You pack your own Chute". The first time I saw it was at Uncle Clair's in St. Louis. Then a few years later, I saw it at a Real Estate motivation meeting in New Orleans.

Eden invited us over for a Birthday party for Atlee. We enjoyed meeting and visiting with the relation again. Shortly after our visit her brother Atlee passed away. His wife, Bobby, still lives there. It was good that we got the chance to visit with Atlee again before he died.

Claud and I went on a trip to Australia. The first thing we did was to go to the Great Barrier Reef. We got on a boat to go to the reef. The reef is under a man made island in the ocean. The reef is 1,240 Miles long and has 500 Species of many colored Coral. When we got there, People were swimming, snorkeling, going down in a small Submarine to see the sea under water; some were going around in a Glass Bottom boat. We mostly enjoyed seeing the fish and urchins under the water, and eating. We took turns going down in the small Submarine and then the Glass Bottom boat. We spent the whole day there and left before dark.

I enjoyed the zoo in Australia. There were five kinds of Kangaroos, a small one, medium size and a large size, and two that lived in trees. You never hear about the other ones, just the big ones. Seeing the Koala's are so cute. I had always called them Koala Bears, I was corrected real quickly. They are NOT Bears. That is like saying they are dog cats, they are two different animals. We did not go to the rain forest area. With my Asthma I was afraid it wouldn't be my thing to do.

While we were in Sidney we went through the Sidney Opera House. They have five separate Auditoriums that can have performing programs at the same time. Right beside the Opera House is the Big Bridge. Only one couple of our group went over it. It's a big long bridge!

The Sidney Harbor is really pretty. They had lots of boats and sail boats. We went on a ride on a big sailboat. The Captain asked if any one wanted to steer the boat. Yes, I did and one guy did. We had 44 on the tour. There were only two of us from Texas, Claud & Me.

Claud and I went through the Veterans' Museum. They had everyone's name in it that died in World War 2. I am so thankful both of my husbands' made it through the war.

In the country they had huge Termite mounds. They were as big as a table but rounded. There were several of them. I had never seen a Termite mound before. The termites around here just ate the wood in houses. One time I was showing a nice house while I was working in Real Estate. I leaned against the wood, and it caved in a little. I turned around and touched the wood and it was just paint in the shape of where they used to have wood. I showed the buyers and left. Later I called the sellers and told them what happened. They said they didn't know about the termites in the home, but they thanked me for calling and telling them.

We had a couple in our group that wanted to get married. The Hotel went all out for them. They rolled out the red carpet for them to walk on. They put big plants on each side of them, The Bride and Groom, Preacher, Best man and Bridesmaid. Most of them were with our tour group. Then we all went to the restaurant for dinner.

New Zealand is a pretty country. When you are walking on the sidewalk you could have a light weight sweater on, and look at the beautiful snow on the mountains.

While we were in New Zealand two couples of us stayed with a family in their home. I think the man in our family to stay with was with the Chamber of Commerce in New Zealand. It was a beautiful home on the golf course. They had big windows all around the living room so you could see the golf course and scenery in three directions... They heated the upstairs with a wood burning stove. We ate dinner in their dining room. It was lamb, mashed potatoes, with a cream pitcher of gravy for all of us, corn, salad, rolls, and for desert we had their country's cake. It was made mostly with crusty whipped egg whites beaten stiff. They served coffee, I had water. One lady asked for more coffee. The Hostess jumped up and made another cup of instant coffee.

We all slept down stairs. There was no heat down stairs. I am used to taking my shower at night. I took the shower and called for Claud to turn down the bed; I ran and climbed in bed before I froze. I asked him to get in bed and hold me. I was cold.

The bath room was two rooms. The toilet was a long hall, just wide enough to go and to wash your hands. The toilet had 2 buttons on top of the stool, one for a half flush and one for a full flush. This was to save water. I was impressed with the flush system. It saved a lot of water. The shower was a separate room; it was a nice large shower.

They had a beautiful Botanic Garden at Christ Church. It had the most beautiful flowers, trees, and all the grounds were beautiful.

One of the things that surprised me was the deer. They raise deer and sell them to United States. The Deer there did not jump! They keep them in a pasture like we do our cows. They did not jump the fences. This surprised me because the deer in America jumped. They also grew trees to sell to the United States.

We took a boat ride to the Walter Peak Sheep Station. The water was real cold, they said if you fell in the water you might not survive because it was so cold. The only way to it is by boat. They had all kinds of animals there.

The guide told the little kids to run up the hill and bring the sheep back down the hill. Several kids took off running. After all the kids started running up to the sheep, one little boy started up all by himself. He had just gone a short distance and the man blew his whistle and yelled for them to come back down. When they got back down he blew his whistle and told the dogs to go get the sheep. Then he caught one sheep and sheered it. There were Elk, an

Australia long hair cow, and some other animals but I don't remember what they were called. We all ate at the restaurant then got back on the boat and headed home. We sang all the way back.

Our next stop was Fiji. Fiji is a very poor country. We visited a commune there. We were told that we had to take our shoes off because we were being entertained in a sacred building. There were no seats. Half of the room was lined with benches for the Company, the rest sit on the floor. We were told that we would be served some of the Native drink. If we did not want any, all we had to do was look down when it is offered. I looked down and he passed by me, then I looked up and he ran back to give me some. I shook my head no and he went on. I had tried it the night before in the restaurant at dinner. It was terrible. One man in our group offered to sit with the head man on the floor and drink it. It was offered to everyone. The men came in first and sit on the floor, and then the women came in and sit on the floor in back of the men. Everyone was offered some of the drink. One old man took a drink and made an awful face. He didn't like it and he probably had drank it all of his life.

This was a commune and everyone had their own little house. The men just fished, and they were gone most of the day. When they did get home they divided the fish with all the residents. The women did most of the other work. They made and sold jewelry. I bought a black set, neck lass and ear rings. They took care of the house and the kids. There was only one refrigerator in the whole commune. Everyone could use it if they needed something to keep several days.

While we were at the hotel Claud was talking to one of the waiters. Claud told him that in Missouri the lake turns over sometimes. The water got real muddy and the fish would not bite until the water cleared up again. He had never heard of this. He asked Claud if he could think about this happening. The next morning the man came up to Claud and said he had figured it out. God had done this, it was a miracle.

We visited the 4th grade in one of their schools. Most of the boys wanted to be a soldier. It was a poor area and the Army would take care of their needs. The girls chose to be a school teacher, or a nurse. There main income was Tourists', Sugar Cane, Corn & Tapioca. Tapioca is grown on bushes under the ground, on a root. As we were leaving the school, two older boys were standing there watching us leave. I said Hello, and shook their hands. I headed on toward the bus, then I looked back to see if Claud was coming. I saw the two boys just standing there looking at their hands. They had probably never touched an American woman before.

The American Legion from the USA built their Schools. The Rotary in America built their hospital. Schools are not mandatory but most of the parents want their children to have an education. The children sang us an American song before we left.

Claud shopped for a hat every place looking for the perfect cap. He finally found it in Fiji. He was so happy to find his cap. When we got home we went to see the kids. We stopped at Dexter's. He took us out for lunch. We left the restaurant and went about a block when Claud remembered he left his cap. He returned but they said they had not seen his cap. No one had seen it anywhere. Someone else liked Claud's cap and kept it.

While we were at the Hotel in Figi, they asked if anyone wanted to go play golf. Several said yes, they wanted to play. So they left, when they got back they told us about their golf game. They were taken by bus to a field; they were given one golf ball to each man, and one golf club. Now they could play golf. The weeds were about knee deep. The bus brought them back to the hotel. I don't think any of them enjoyed their golf game.

One of our trips was going through the Panama Canal. I told Oliver that we were going on this trip. A big group of us were going from Adobe Wells. Oliver and Shirley wanted to go too. I told him what it costs and come on if they really wanted to go. Oliver and Shirley went with us. There were 82 of us that went together. I took a picture of our group. We were beside the Queen Elisabeth ship going through the Panama Canal. Two ships can go through the Canal at the same time. When we were up, the QE2 was down. They were just a little ahead of us. We kept waving to their ship and they were all waving back. The two ships stayed fairly close until we disbanded at Acapulco.

They were still first in line. While we waited to disembark, the people dropped coins from the boat in the ocean for the native kids to catch. I learned something else. The coins just kind of float down with the coins flat, so the kids can catch them pretty easy. This was a very informative trip for me.

In 2002 we went to the Woods & DuBois Family Reunion. We got an invitation to stay with Monroe [Sticks] and Phyllis Rowland's home. Claud enjoyed the reunion so much. He had not seen any of his Family from Massachusetts for a long time. There were 60 that attend the Dinner. I helped Phyllis fix every body Breakfast on the last day before they left for home. Monroe cooked Johnny Cakes. Its thin dough fried like a skinny pancake. You roll it up and eat it hot or you can put Jelly or syrup on it. We all visited the Fall River Historical Society. They had a whole room about the DuBois's. One was a sea Captain of a Steamship. His dishes had their DuBois sign on them. They had a lot about the Captain of the ship. Fall River was his home.

I asked Phyllis why she picked us to stay in her house. She answered, "I knew who would help me fix breakfast." Really they were just so glad to see Claud.

We left Rowland's home and planned to stop in New Jersey to visit Claud's Aunt. She called just before we left and said don't come.

They were expecting a Hurricane. The traffic had picked up as people were going further away from the coast. It was bumper to bumper traffic and raining. We just got to Pennsylvania and I suggested that we stop. Claud said no not yet. He wanted to go to a town just a little further. We did stop where he wanted to stop. The next morning when we got up, there were tree's that had lost branches lying all around, but no big damage. Claud was right again.

Some of the other places we had the pleasure to visiting, and seeing was Venezuela, Barbados, Puerto Rico, San Juan, St. Thomas, and Curacas. When we docked in Caracas I looked out the balcony, it was so pretty. Not like all the other Islands. I said "Oh Claud, get up! This place is so pretty."

Later, I said something about it to our guide. He said the Mayer of the town, asked everyone to paint their property. The fact that he owned the paint company might have something to do with it. Each owner had painted everything they owned one color. The house, garage, fence, sheds, every thing matched all through town. But they were all different colors, and so clean. We have always enjoyed our trips.

One evening Claud took Tiger for his night walk. I heard a knock on the door. When I answered it, it was one of the neighbors. He said Claud was lying on the side of the road. I ran out, and then called the Ambulance. I followed it to the hospital. He had broken a bone on his hip. He was in the Hospital and was doing real well healing.

Maxine came to visit with her Dad, but she did not have much time, so she couldn't stay very long. Kenneth came for a short visit while Claud was in the hospital. Then he went to visit some relatives for the evening.

One time when I got to the hospital, Claud had a catheter in him. I asked why and they said he had not urinated for three days. I told them that had happened before. He needed an Urologist to come and ream him out. They said OK, they would tell the Doctor.

Three days later, he had one in him again. I went to the desk and told them again. The third time they put the catheter in him he hollered, it hurt him and he had gotten infection. It spread fast. The Doctor told me there was no hope. The infection had spread too much through his body. I couldn't believe that they didn't do what I asked them to do for him. I didn't know that they would not call the Urologist for Claud. I feel terrible because I didn't realize that I should have called the Urologist myself. Why didn't the Doctor or nurse tell me I had to call. I really loved Claud and I let him down.

Claud died January 3, 2009 in McAllen, Texas. Claud and I were married a little over eleven wonderful happy years. We were married March 14, 1998, and he died January 3, 2009. Claud was 87 years old and would have been 88 on February 2, 2009. Claud was in great shape, he felt good and everything was ok. Until he went to the hospital. Claud was liked by everyone.

We had his Memorial at our church and again at our Club House in Adobe Wells. Dexter & Carol came down. Kenneth, Bonna and their daughter came down. While people were still there, Kenneth asked if Dexter could unlock the house so he could get their luggage and go home.

When I came back home, Kenneth had his truck loaded. All except the Princess picture that I had already told him he could not have. It was promised to Maxine because Kenneth had taken the harbor picture that their Mother had painted. They argued with me and said Claud had promised Bonna that picture. I knew he did not, and I told him again that picture went to Maxine. He took it any way and put it in his truck.

I was tempted to call the police. He stole it. The will was worded that the house and everything in it goes to Twylia. I felt so bad about Kenneth stealing it. I told Maxine and she didn't seem surprised at all.

Claud and I went to bed every night, and we talked about his life, the army, the farm in New Hampshire, every thing. I really loved that man and he loved me. I knew it, I felt his love, and I miss him so much.

After Claud died I had a hard time for awhile. I missed him so much because we did about everything together. The rest of 2009 just kind of flew by. This is one of my favorite pictures of Claud and his smile.

Claud and I had planned to go on a Caribbean cruise before he died. Murl Gustafson and I decided to go on the cruise because it was already planned and already paid for. It was just a week cruise. I don't even remember much about it. The south end of the cruise was Barbados.

I was in charge of Trips at the Club house. I planned a short day trip to Port Isabel. It was real good. We went through two museums, those that wanted to went up the light house. We took a trolley ride all through Port Isabel. The ship yards, the live sea museum, ate at the restaurant right by the bridge going into Padre Island. Fourteen ladies went on the trip; it turned into a real nice trip, even if it did rain on us.

We had a Ladies luncheon at the Vantage Café in McAllen. Everyone was dressed in old fashion clothes and hats. The Café had a lot to pick from. It was a fun day for about 27 ladies.

Violet Roberson and I decided to go on a three week cruise to Canada. Violet had lost her husband too. Violet had a friend, Norma Krampitz, from California that wanted to go with us. She flew to Huston and we got together at Violet's home in Houston. We flew to Fort Lauderdale to start the trip; it was a three week trip ending in Montreal Canada. We stopped in Newport, Bar Harbor, Nova Scotia, and Sydney where they make Violins. We stopped in many ports but I can't remember all the other Ports.

One place six French Men sang and danced for us in costume and entertained us on the dock. We were all leaning over the railing to see and hear them. After they quit singing one man and his wife came on board to see the ship. His wife took Violet and my picture with him in his complete costume.

The ship decorated and put on a Chocolate display. Two big tables of different things chocolate were on display. They sure looked good; we all wanted some of it. Two nights later, after everyone got to see and enjoy looking at all that good chocolate, they threw it all away. They wouldn't let anyone have any because it had sat out on display for two days. It was not sanitary.

At another place on a river, we were the first ship to ever stop in their town. They closed the shops, let out school and everyone met us at the dock. That was pretty exciting and fun. After they greeted us, it was business as usual. I wish I could remember the name of that town. We stayed there about two hours.

We started home from Quebec, Canada on the air plane. After flying awhile they announced that there was some trouble and we were going to make an emergency landing. I don't remember the small town. When we stopped, we were completely surrounded by the emergency fire trucks, police and etc. We sit in the plane for about an hour. They decided that we could go into the airport until they decided what to do with us.

They finally took us to a Hotel, we checked into a room and they left us. We had nothing to eat since breakfast and it was now about eleven at night. There were four of us, Norma, Violet, a man and me. We walked to a restaurant about 3 blocks from us and they were locking the door. They would not let us in. So we walked a few more blocks to Hooters. It was full of college age kids, it was loud, but they had food! The kids made room for us by some of them doubling up. They were all nice to these old people. The waitress came to us and they had made a table just for us. Just across from us was the designated driver. We talked and told him of all of our plane problems. After we ate, Violet asked him if we could pay him to take us back to the Hotel. He said NO, but he would be glad to take us. What a thoughtful and kind young man. We got on a plane the next day and made it back to Houston to Violets and I caught the plane the next morning to Dallas..

I still travel to see the kids each year. I stop to see them going and coming back home. It is usually a 3 week trip. This year Murl traveled with me. She is from Adobe Wells too. We stopped in Dallas to see Carol and Peggy. We stayed overnight with them. It was a 10 hour drive. We stopped over night and visited with Leonard and Ruann Clinesmith in Eufaula, Oklahoma.

We stopped in to visit with Cora and John Coventon in Muskogee, Oklahoma. Then we went on to see Polly and Rich, Erik, Lacey, Eli, and Samatha, We stayed overnight with Polly and Family in Nixa, MO.

We stayed all night with Dexter and we all visited with Marjorie and her family in Jefferson City, Missouri.

Marjorie was Lloyd's sister, we always got along so well, and I always felt she was my sister. Marjorie had cancer; she doctored for it and is in remission. I hope and pray it does not come back.

Our next stop was to visit Jerry and Melissa in Creve Coeur, Missouri. While there we visited several good Friends that we used to know when we lived there. We lived there for 15 years. We had short visits with Lou Belcher, Pat Webb, and Phyllis Walsh. Several friends ate lunch with us.

Maxine Scott, Claud's daughter was in Decatur, Illinois. I took Maxine several boxes of things that was Claud's or at least from his home. She was so thrilled to get the stuff. I think what she enjoyed most was a hanging plate with a picture of their farm in New Hampshire on it. She cried when she saw it. I really like Claud's daughter. She has raised her four girls by herself. She works pretty hard and has raised some pretty nice kids. I don't think her husband ever gave her any help with money. He married again but she has not yet.

We started back home, stopping over night at Jerry's again. We stopped in Muskogee, Oklahoma. Cora and John Coventon lived there. John was not feeling his best but they were glad to see us.

We stopped over night to see Peggy, Carol and Danny again. It was a good trip but glad to be back in McAllen again. All together I drove 2758 Miles. We made it home with no car trouble.

I guess I should tell you about being stopped by the Police. As we were leaving Illinois, there were several little towns fairly close together. I kept slowing down but maybe not quite enough. So I was pulled over. The Police man said, "You were going to fast through that town." "Where are you going in such a hurry?" I said, "We are going clear to Texas." He laughed. "Well, I won't give you a ticket this time, but don't drive so fast, and don't tell any one that I let you go". I told him, "I would have to tell my son. He would get a kick out of me getting stopped." The Police man said "OK tell your son but no one else". He started to turn away but stopped and looked back at me. He said "You were going to fast on this road too". God does take care of me. I did slow down.

I stayed in Adobe Wells after Claud died for a year and ½. I just was not ready to move. I had wonderful Friends there.

When I decided to move to Frisco, I sold the house in a week. Violet and I had planned to go to Padre Island for a week before I moved. I told Carol and Danny and they asked if they could go to Padre Island too. I said we didn't care but there was only one bed and a couch in the living room. Violet and I got the bed. Danny brought an air mattress for them. The first night the air all leaked out. Carol slept on the couch and Danny slept on the no air mattress. Carol and Danny spent a lot of time sun bathing on the beach.

Violet and I could not get in the water, so we were pretty much staying inside. Violet was going to have an operation. I had turned and hit the corner of the treadmill with my leg as I was packing. It dug a big hole in my leg. It took 4 months to heal. The Doctor said not to bandage it any more. Let the air get to it and it will heal much faster.

We rented a truck, loaded it and Danny drove the truck, Carol drove their car, and I drove my car. We had a nice little train driving to Frisco. I left so much of my stuff. Some I hadn't planned to leave.

I moved into an apartment Number 1309, one the third floor. I have nice two bedroom apartment with two baths, a small dining area, living room, kitchen, and a nice balcony. I got moved in with Danny and Carol's help. Danny hung all my pictures with Carols' help. I made it a point to get acquainted as fast as I could. Each night at dinner I would sit with someone that I had not met before. Slowly, I did get pretty well acquainted with most of the people.

I live pretty close to Carol; she is only about 10 minutes away. Peggy lives in Carrolton; it is a little further away, maybe a half hour. Jeffrey, Kelly and Sean are real close. They live in the next subdivision.

Vera and Ben live in Texas City. We always enjoy visiting with Vera. She is fun to be with. We spent a Christmastime with Vera and her whole family several years ago. Everyone exchanged gifts. Vicky's husband, Kenny Mills fixed all of us a wonderful meal. He's a good cook. They have a nice house and swimming pool.

Now I have made many friends, I started Bridge here; I gave lessons to ones that wanted to learn. Now we have about 100 that know how but some of them don't play very often. When I came they did not have any organized games but bingo. Now we have about every game you can think of playing.

I went back to McAllen to visit Mary Jane about a year after I had moved here. It was a great visit but Adobe Wells was not the same. Mary Jane sold her home and moved back to Rushville, Indiana. Swede had died. Betty and Wayne moved back to their home in North Dakota. The Howard and Delores Armentrouts moved to be near their daughter in Pearland, Texas, part of Houston. About a year after they moved Howard died. Sue Johnson and Dick moved near his daughter in Beloit, Wisconsin. After they moved Dick died. Sue moved to Phoenix, Arizona, she is living with her daughter and Granddaughter.

One year Danny got us tickets to attend the Horse Races, we bet but I don't think anyone was a big winner. I know I didn't, but it was good to be all together.

They had the best fire works I had ever seen. Kelly, Sean, Noah, Sophia, Jeffrey, Carol, Danny and me. We played games, played with the kids, visited and it was a fun evening.

We had Thanksgiving Day one year with Polly & Family in Nixa. Dexter & Jerry came to Polly's to be with us too. We all had a great time, played games, and visited. I raised a game playing Family.

One of our Christmas vacations was spent on a 5 day cruise with Carol, Danny, Peggy, Jeffrey, Kelly, Sean, Noah, Sophie, Sousan, Bruce, Ava, and me. We all had a good time. But for me, it didn't seem like Christmas.

It was nice and fun to be with the family. We went to see the shows in the evening.

I remembered the great times we had at the Lake of the Ozarks. Those were the good old days. The kids enjoyed the lake as much as Lloyd and I did. It was a great place for my family. We played in the lake in the day time. Then we played cards and games each evening.

Every two years we have a Clinesmith Reunion. We always stayed at Raymond, my cousin, and Mary Pearls' home. When Oliver and Calvin, Raymond's brother, was alive, Oliver always stayed with Calvin and Rena. I also enjoyed being with Raymond and Mary when they were Winter Texans too. They make home made Ice Cream. Violet and I went to the last Reunion in Buffalo. We stayed a week in Branson. Then went on to Betty and Harry Brunks. They invited us to stop over and stay all night with them in Arma, Kansas.

We followed Betty and Harry on to Coyvillle and enjoyed the McVey Family reunion. After visiting for awhile we went on to Raymond and Marys. It was a lot of driving for me but I didn't mind it at all. I have always enjoyed the Family reunions. I don't know if I will get to go to the next one or not. The kids don't want me to drive that far gain. I have had no trouble on any of my trips. I enjoy visiting with the family' s that come. Kenneth Jarvis came last time and brought a girl friend. I always enjoy visiting with Raymnd and Mary.

I got acquainted pretty quickly here in Stonebrook Parkway, Frisco, Texas. I wanted to play Bridge so I got busy and organized a Bridge group.

A lot of the people at Parkview had played bridge a long time ago. Some just wanted to learn. So I gave bridge lessons to teach and refresh the ones that had forgotten how to play. It has grown, a lot of new friends moved into Parkview. A lot of them played bridge so we have bridge on Monday, Wednesday and Friday now. We have party bridge and now we are having Duplicate Bridge two days a month.

Violet Roberson, Rita Hammond, and I went to Rome in 2011. We met Violet at her house and flew out the next morning. We flew from Houston to London, then on to Rome. We got on the Costa Cruise ship. The first stop was Palermo [Sicily], that's an Island at the foot of Rome. We spent the day sight seeing. The second day we went to Cagliari Island in Sardinia. I had never heard of this Island before. More sight seeing. Then we went to Spain. Palma de Mallorca, then Barcelona, we really enjoyed Barcelona. The streets were so narrow. We could hardly get down a street, we were afraid the cab would hit something. We rode on the big double layer bus and went all through the town. We went to a big bull fight ring. We saw a lot of beautiful buildings. There were several parades in all different kinds of customs.

We went to France next. Marseille was interesting too. We went by cab and looked at everything there. Then we went to Savona & on to Rome in Italy.

We saw the Vatican palace. We did not see him. They pointed his bedroom out to us. Another girl that we met did see him. She was given a branch and she shared it with us. There were a lot of pictures of the grounds, the buildings, and the people that lived there in older times.

The beautiful art work on the ceiling that Michael Angelo painted was fantastic. They were down the whole hallway.

We checked out St. Peter's Basilica. The old one had been replaced because of age, and wear. Saint Peter, the chief apostle, was buried in 64 A.D. We took the panoramic tour all over the town on a double deck bus again. We missed our spot to get off the bus. I asked what we do now. We were told to get on the subway. It was not far from where we had to go. A painter and a lady helped us to know where to get off. The man was carrying a big picture that he had painted. But they didn't tell us which way to go after we got off. After asking someone every step of the way, we got back to our hotel.

The Spanish steps. There were a zillion of them. There were just too many. I did not climb them but I enjoyed seeing them.

The Coliseum was straight down from our Hotel room. We decided to walk to it. Bad idea, it was right down our street but it took forever. I keep forgetting that I am getting older.

The Coliseum was probably is the most impressive building of the Roman Empire. It was the largest building of the era. Just parts of it are still there. Down inside the building there were different areas where the people were waiting for their part in the show. They also kept the bulls down here too. I didn't like seeing them hurt the bulls by sticking sharp swards in the bulls to make them mad. I have never seen a Matador in a bull ring with a bull but I didn't want to see the bull or the Matador get killed.

When we finally got down the hill to the Coliseum, we went into a little restaurant to have a bit of lunch. Violet said she wanted a Margareta so we all three got one. We were enjoying ourselves and a young couple from Brazil started talking with us. Then she wanted to take our picture. Then another lady across the room came over and wanted to take our picture. I guess we were silly Americans. But we were enjoying our selves. Oh Yes, before we left to on with our sightseeing, we decided we all should go to the bathroom. It was down stairs.

The Ladies restroom was closed so everyone used the men's. It felt kind of funny, there would be a couple of men in line, and then a couple of ladies, there were about eleven in line. It took awhile.

Rita walked all around the Coliseum; she got lost trying to get out but finally made it back to our room. Rita is in her 60's. Violet and I were in our 80's. We didn't go everywhere that Rita went. It was just too much walking.

We had an elevator going up to our room. It was big enough for two. It had two buttons, one up and one down. We had a nice big room. We each had our own bed. Before we left home I was a little concerned about Rita's health. She has to take her machine to help her sleep. Her breathing wasn't real good either. [Mine either], and just before we left home, her leg was hurting her and she couldn't walk very well. But we all made it just fine. I have always said "Where there is a will, there is a way".

We took a taxi back to the airport, heading back to London, then to Houston. We had not been seated in the plane long when the man seated next to me spilled his coffee on me. We were on the plane leaving London. I ran to the Restroom, grabbed some paper towels to try to dry off. I was completely wet clear down. One of the men that worked on the plane gave me a complete set of their work uniforms. It was all black with their plane emblem on it. I still have it but it is way too big, but it kept me dry. We stayed at Violets that night. Rita and I got the plane the next morning and flew back to Dallas. Danny picked us up at the airport. It was a good trip and it felt good to get home again.

Carol and Danny had a big Luau in their back yard. It was really a good party. The next day, Carol and Danny helped me put on a Luau in their back yard. It worked great; we used the same decorations and some of the same food.

I asked Molly, the head of our apartments, if we could use the Parkview Bus? So most of my guests came on the bus and Don came back to get them after the party. I had about 12, not counting Carol, Danny, Peggy and me. Everyone said that it was the party of the year. I had a lot of help and it was a great party.

Violet went with me to Branson again this year. I invited Tom and Bettye Gault from Overland Park, Kansas on Sunday and Monday to come to Branson and visit with Violet and me. Then I invited Marshall and Beth Lett from Pineville, Missouri to come on Tuesday and Wednesday, then Betty and Harry Brunk from Arma, Kansas to come and visit Thursday and Friday. It worked real well and we had a good visit with each of them. We had to leave on Saturday. Friday evening Violet and I went to one of the Branson shows.

Not every day is great. My Parents death was hard on me. My husband Lloyd died after 48 ½ years, He had cancer of the Pancreas. My brother Oliver has been gone 8 years, He had Leukemia. My husband Claud has been gone almost 5 years. I miss each and every one of them. It was so hard when my son Jim died of Cancer. He has been gone 9 years now. Then I lost my youngest son Dexter with Sugar Diabetes. He has been gone 4 years. It is Gods will but it is still hard.

Two years have passed since our last Family Reunion. It is about time for us all to get together again. Violet is going with me again. I will be driving, I'm only 81 but I will be 82 by the time I get home again. We will be staying a week in Branson again. Then we are going to visit Betty & Harry over night at their home in Arma, Kansas. Then Violet and I will be going to the McVey Family Reunion in Coyville, Kansas. They always have a big lunch and we have a great visit with all of their family. I always enjoy visiting with Vera and her family. Later we went on to Raymond and Mary Clinesmith's home for the rest of the Clinesmith Reunion.

It is always on a Saturday and Sunday. Saturday is something surprising and fun. Sunday is lunch and visiting. They have begun to just price the Sunday dinner and we pay whatever it costs. That is much easier than having to take something when you live so far away.

The younger generation has taken over the programs. One year we had a pit and they cooked a calf in the pit, another year it was a shrimp boil, my favorite was a trip to my Great Grandparents home place. A tractor pulled the hay wagon and we all rode on the big wagon. It is fun, you never know what they will think of next.

Each year I take my Family Tree Book. The relatives look through it and read about their part of the family history.

The good news this year is that Peggy and Craig Whealy are engaged. Her ring is beautiful. It has a square setting with a big diamond in the middle, and a line of diamonds on each side of the ring. It is very pretty.

Peggy moved in with Craig after they got engaged. So she is not here now. I miss her. She is working for him. He has an office but he did not have any files. He just had everything in boxes. She bought a comfortable chair, a desk, a file cabinet and started to work.

I do really enjoy being here at Stonebrook Parkway in Frisco. It is an Independent Living Adults place to live. I do not cook; I eat in the dining room and order whatever I want to eat. I have a maid every Wednesday morning at 8 A.M.; I do have to do my own laundry. Where else could I retire and not have to do anything?

We have started a Welcome committee to visit with the new people when they first move in. We show them the place and introduce them to other residents. We are putting out a quarterly Resident News Paper. One of my jobs is to be a roving Reporter. I interviewed some of the residents about their life. They are all so interesting. I interviewed four residents in the first News Paper, Susan Hall, Mel Hillert, Richard & Helen Rowe, and Betty Silk. We will be putting out another News Letter in three months. This is a fun job.

Carol, Danny, Kelly and Jeffrey live fairly close to me. I love it when they come over. Also it is wonderful when Kelly brings Noah & Sophia, my Great Grandchildren over for a visit. Kelly used to come over every Wednesday morning. We had lunch here or we went out to lunch to McDonalds or to Taco Bell. Both places have a great play area for the little kids. Kelly said that she never got to know her Great Grand Parents and she wanted her kids to know the ones left. It's a good life. They always give me a big hug or I guess I should say they let me hug them.

Peggy is working for Craig. She got his office all set up so they now can find the information and know where to look. Craig works for Meridian Forestry. His office is in Groveton, Texas. He lives in Lovelady, Texas in the country. They are 24 miles North of Crocket. Craig's Mother is Claire Whealy. She lives in Tulsa, Oklahoma.

Peggy and Craig came and we all got together for Christmas at Carol and Danny's home. They stayed with Carol for 2 nights. Then Claire, Craig's mother, flew in from Tulsa, Oklahoma. They brought his Mother over to meet Peggy's Family and spend Christmas with all of us. They all stayed in our guest suite. It is quite plush. They liked it there. We had 13 at Carol's for Christmas dinner. They were Carol, Danny, Jeffrey, Stacy, Kelly, Sean, Peggy, Craig, Claire, Twylia, Kayleigh, Noah & Sophia. Then later Bruce, Sousan, Sean's sister, Ava, her boyfriend, his parents and his brother. That makes 20 altogether.

We had a super bonus. It snowed. The snow was so pretty and it is great to have snow at Christmas time. Danny tried to show the kids how to make a snowman. Noel just wanted to throw snow and make a pile of snow. So Danny gave up on the snow man.

Craig, Peggy and Claire had breakfast here with me in the dining room. They stayed over night in the Parkview apartment that you can reserve for your company. Then they came to my apartment to visit and wait until time to take Claire to the airport. Peggy and Craig took his Mom to the airport to fly back to Tulsa, Oklahoma where she lives. Then Peggy and Craig started home to Lovelady, Texas. Peggy called me about 5:30 P.M. to tell me they were home. I love it when one of the kids is so thoughtful, I just feel better when I know they made it home again.

A Tornado went close by their home while they were here. The generator went out but there didn't seem to be any other trouble. Peggy called this morning and said she was on the way to Craig's office. Peggy is helping him in the office. She said "He really needed me". Craig works mostly outdoors doing his Forestry thing. Craig has two horses, one mule, five cows, two dogs beside Peggy's little Molly. They just had an addition in their family. Ginger is a tiny white Chihuahua only about a month old.

January 4, 2013 was Danny's 64th Birthday. He took his whole family and me out for a big dinner at B.J. Chung's restaurant. Carol, Danny, Jeffrey, Stacy, Keyleigh, Kelly, Sean, Noah, Sophia and I, there were ten of us all together. It was a fun evening. Carol and Danny are both very good to me.

Jan. 23rd, Mel, Lou and I went through the Cowboy Stadium. There was no game on at that day so we went on a great tour. I was very impressed. Everything was so thought out for several different activities. They have five different fields. One field for the ball games, one field for Rodeo's, [they put several thickness of dirt down and after the rodeo is over they take all the dirt up and put it in storage to use again], each different event requires different ground. They have lots of storage space.

They had huge television screens all around the stadium. The seats are arranged by prices. The Special box's was plush, Then they had the padded seats, the cheaper ones are good wood molded seats. They have lots of places to eat your hot dogs and whatever you want.

On March 30, 2013 four of us Ladies were going on a Paddle Boat Cruise for a week. Barbara, Susie, Lydia and I were going to fly from Dallas to New Orleans. The tour started in New Orleans, then went to Memphis, Tennessee. The boat was a Paddle boat and it had about four decks. I learned that a boat on the river was a boat. On the ocean it would have been a ship. When it was time to go Susie Hall did not get to go. When the tour was over, we flew back home to Dallas. We were all looking forward to the trip when Susie couldn't go and there were only three of us. I guess we just as well have fun while we can!

Tom and Betty Gault moved into a place like Parkview about three months ago. Betty called me and told me that Tom was having some problems. But he did like living in their apartment. A few days later Bettye called me and told me the Tom had died.

She sent me a tape they made of Tom's life. It is a great tape. It was about his Family and Friends. Lloyd and I were in it several times because we were good friends and went on many trips together. Tom was always happy and fun to be with I will miss him. I have invited Betty to come and visit with me, I hope she does come.

I am adding this later...Susie was visiting her son and started to sit on one of those high bar stools. She slipped and fell. It bruised her leg real badly. She did not get to go with us on the trip. Her leg took about 3 months to heal. They had to cut a spot on her leg so the matter could get out of her leg and it could heal. The three of us did go on the trip. We had a great time, but wished Susie could have gone with us. We met several new friends that did play bridge. We had about three tables when we could all get together.

I just got an e-mail from Sue Johnson in Arizona, she said she hadn't heard from me, and asked if I was OK. I called her back and we talked for quite a while. She told me her Granddaughter had her first date! That is always a big deal for the parents and the girl. The kids met at the Ice Cream place, ate ice cream and talked.

Sue got a new washing machine. She cleaned where it used to set. It had water under it; she said she was surprised to find a cricket swimming in the water. That made me laugh, I have never seen a cricket swim.

Sue hadn't lived with her daughter in Arizona very long when a small hole came up in her yard. In two weeks the sink hole grew covering about a fourth of the yard; it stopped just about 3 feet from her bedroom. She had two big loads of gravel hauled in and filled the sink hole. I asked her if she had any more trouble with the sink hole. She said no. Now her yard is just pretty grass again.

July 25, 2013 was my birthday. I am now 83; I do not feel 83, everyone says I do not look 83, but it is a fact. I am 83 today! It was a very happy day for me. The children came to eat my Birthday dinner with me. There was 8 adults and 3 children, Carol, Danny, Jeff, Stacey, Kayleigh, Kelly, Sean, Noah, Sophia, and Peggy. Peggy drove about four hours to come and eat dinner with me. She stayed all night with me and then drive 4 more hours going back home. When she called me to tell me she was coming, I cried after I hung up, she is so thoughtful. I said at breakfast that morning that I was having 10 come for my Birthday. The girls at my table got together and donated meals for all my guests. Good Friends are wonderful. They always come through when they are needed.

Jerry, my son, called from St. Louis and we visited for about a half hour on the phone. I love it when the kids call me. I never know when the kids have time for me to talk with them. Polly called from Nixa and we visited for a little while. It was a wonderful Birthday. Sometimes people raise their eye-brows when I say I have six children. I love each and everyone of them. As you get older, you love and appreciate them more and more.

Lacey, my Granddaughter, planned and arranged everything for her wedding herself. The wedding was on Saturday, July 27th at 6 P.M. in the Hopedale Baptist Church in Ozark, Missouri. The invitation was from, Lacey Marie Leffler and James Bradley Middleton. The night before the wedding we all arrived in Nixa in time to go to the groom's dinner. The dinner was in his parents' home. We met several of James family and friends. Jim and Ronda Middleton, his parents, are real nice. We had a nice visit with each of them, they are Teachers. They have a nice place on about an acre of yard. James is a real nice young man. I think he and Lacey will be a happy, religious couple.

The next morning we, all the girls went early to the church to get ready. They finished with the decorations.

Jerry and Melissa met us at the motel. We were all ready to go to the wedding. Danny was driving. He had gotten the directions, however someway we got lost. We called for directions again. We got our new directions and this time we found the right church. We were late but "They waited for us!"

Lacey looked great in her beautiful white wedding dress, and Polly looked beautiful in her new purple dress. Samatha was the brides maid, and Eli and Erik ware ushers. I told Rich that he looked really good in his Tux. Peggy said she cut and fixed every one's hair, she had just visited with them for a week. Each and everyone looked really nice.

Carol french braded Lacey's hair in the back and fixed big curls in the front. I took pictures of every one getting ready for the wedding. It was fun for me to be there with Lacey, Samatha, Polly and Carol. Even if I am a whole Generation older, I loved being included.

James had friends that played the music. James and Lacey danced the first dance, then the four parents joined them. After the first dance several joined the dancing.

Ronda and her friends fixed a delightful refreshment table. James threw the garter for his buddies to catch. Lacey threw the bouquet and a little girl caught it. I really do not think little kids should be in the group to catch anything. It is not fair to the older girls the brides age.

We all blew bubbles as the Bride and Groom left. It was a real nice wedding. After the wedding we all went to Jerry's room and ate pizza, and visited until about midnight.

Melissa and I had a great visit while being roommates in the hotel. She is such a busy girl, she works full time and is still in College getting her degree. The next day, Sunday, we took out for St. Louis. We visited Kate, Danny's Mother, that evening. We all stayed for a great Kentucky Fried chicken dinner. After dinner we all played poker. That is Kate's favorite card game. That evening Carol and Danny stayed with Kate. I stayed at Jerry's home.

Monday, Jerry, Danny, Carol and I went to play golf. I drove Carol in the golf cart. I didn't play because while we were still in Adobe Wells it hurt my back after I played, so I quit playing. I told them the next time we play golf, I am going to play again to see if it still hurts my back. That night they all came to Jerry's for a good steak dinner, after eating we played poker again.

Tuesday morning we started home. We went by Polly's and Samatha, my Granddaughter, came back to Dallas with us. She stayed with Carol and Danny and had her own bedroom. It gave her a little vacation and we all enjoyed her company.

Danny took Samatha home on his way back to St. Louis. Danny had to go back to St. Louis to help his Mother with some of her finances and to fix her house where there was hail damage. Danny and Jerry put new siding on the west side of Kates house and replaced two windows on the west side of the house.

My Birthday took a small back seat. We were all so excited about the wedding. However I received 42 Birthday cards. I got nine face book birthday greetings, several from friends in Adobe Wells. I also got three phone calls. This just blew my mind, everyone is so wonderful. I wonder if the kids realize how much we love them. I would not be such a happy person, if I didn't have such great kids and friends.

Danny and Carol both play tennis. They went to New York to watch the tennis professionals play off matches. They were there a week.

On Sunday, September 8, 2013, we went to the Schooner II Beach and Racket Club Resort. It is in Myrtle Beach, South Carolina. It is a real nice place; they said on the phone it has a Silver Crown 4 Star rating. I got six reservations for Carol and Danny, Peggy and Craig, Violet and me. We flew to Myrtle Beach, Danny rented a six passenger car for all of us. Danny and Carol had a unit just below the rest of us.

The sand was so deep that Violet and I had a hard time trying to walk in it. It was about six inches deep. I told the kids they would have to help us go and be in the water one day but not yet.

Several days went by and they said today was the day. Violet and I each had a man on one side of us and one of the girls on the other. They walked us clear to the beach and in the water about to the waist but not quite. It was fun.

Violet kept saying further out, a big wave came and caught us. Violet just went rolling, they lost hold of her, the silly girl still wanted to go out further. The two holding her said no, they were taking her back. We sit on the beach for a while, then they helped us back to the regular ground. We both enjoyed just watching the ocean. The sun rising and the sun setting were so pretty.

The next day Peggy and Craig gave us an envelope. Mine said, "MOM". It was an invitation to their wedding. We were all surprised and so happy they included us in their plans.

They got married on the beach. Peggy had arranged all the plans before they left Lovelady. The preacher came and put up an arbor. We all followed walking in the sand. The Minister brought us four chairs. Peggy and Craig were barefooted. They stood under the arbor and repeated their Vowels.

A SPECIAL INVITATION

The wedding uniting Craig Whealy + Peggy Adams
Occasion

Thursday, Sept. 12, 2013 5:00 PM
Date Time

Beachside, North Myrtle Beach, SC
Place

Dinner reservations @ Villa Tuscanna

They exchanged their rings. The Minister pronounced them Man and Wife. Craig kissed Peggy. Craig said he fell in Love with Peggy the first time he saw her. The wedding was so nice. Peggy did a great job of planning the whole wedding from Lovelady. Peggy's dress was beautiful, it was white with shiny white places on the white. I never had seen Craig look so happy he just glowed. Peggy and Craig both looked so happy.

We all walked back on the boardwalk toward the car. We stopped and we all had a Champaign toast to the bride and groom. We took more pictures. Then we got back in the car and went to a nice restaurant to eat dinner. After dinner Peggy and Craig left us and went to a different Hotel. We all got together on Saturday. Violet's son and his family joined us for Saturday lunch before we left on the plane heading home. Peggy was my baby. Now she is married to a real nice man. I have been very fortunate that my children are wonderful adults. I love each and everyone of the children, and they are very caring with me.

One day I was feeling a little sorry for myself. So many of my loved ones have died. I sat down and wrote this little note.

"Is Life Fair?"

"We learn to live with it. If life was fair,
My parents would not have died when I was 10.
My Grandmother would not have been so unfair; boys
could do no wrong and girls, nothing right.
I would not have married so young, mostly to get away from Grandma.
I was very lucky to love and marry such a good man,
but so unfair to have lost him.
I was lucky a second time to find a wonderful man,
but so unfair to have lost him too in just ten years.
I was unlucky to lose my brother, but so lucky to have had him as long as I did.
I was so worried about my son Jim. It was so unfair to lose him to cancer at 52.
My youngest son Dexter had cancer and diabetes; we lost him at age 53.
I was so lucky to have six wonderful children. Each of them so different but great with their own personalities.
I am so lucky to have ten of the best grandchildren in the world. I love each and every one of them.
Life is not fair! But it is wonderful, even with the bad times. Life is balanced with so many blessings, I feel lucky and happy with my life."

Yes, I am blessed. What more could anyone ask for!
Wonderful children and lots of love. I enjoy every day and thank God for a good family and many good friends.
God bless you all.